A Practical Guide for IoT Solution Architects

Architecting secure, agile, economical, highly available, well-performing IoT solutions

Dr Mehmet Yildiz

Distinguished Enterprise Architect

Third Edition, November 2019

Copyright © Dr Mehmet Yildiz

Publisher: S.T.E.P.S. Publishing Australia

Contact Author https://digitalmehmet.com

P.O Box 2097, Roxburgh Park, Victoria, 3064 Australia

info@stepsconsulting.com.au

Second Edition by Mark Longfield

<u>Disclaimer</u>

Table of Contents

Chapter 1 – About the Book

Purpose

I authored this book to provide a simplified practical guide and insightful advice for a selected target group, which we can call 'IoT Solution Architects'. If you search the internet for the term IoT (Internet of Things), you may come across hundreds of publications in the form of books, papers, blogs and other resources about IoT on the market. This book does not repeat the information covered in those publications. It offers a unique perspective and focus based on practical experience.

My purpose is to explain IoT in the simplest possible terms using established architectural framework for creating customised IoT solutions. This is a concise, practical, vendor and technology agnostic solution architecture guide for IoT architects

The framework covers crucial several business concerns that can guide the IoT solution architects that include security, availability, performance, speed to market and cost-effectiveness of the solutions or services at hand.

In the IoT literature, researchers have

stated that these significant concerns are shared by many business executives dealing with IoT products and services. Therefore, in this book, I have reviewed these concerns systematically and presented practical advice to the IoT Solution Architects in terms of how to deal with these concerns using architectural knowledge, skills, and experience.

The focus

The focus of this book is to provide IoT solution architects with simplified practical guidance and a unique perspective. Solution architects working in IoT ecosystems have an unprecedented level of responsibility at work; therefore, dealing with IoT ecosystems can be daunting for many of us.

As an experienced practitioner of this topic, I understand the challenges faced by the IoT solution architects. Thereby, I have reflected upon my insights based on my solution architecture experience spread across three decades. In addition, this book can also guide other architects and designers who want to learn the architectural aspects of IoT and understand the key challenges and practical resolutions in

IoT solution architectures. Each chapter focuses on the key aspects that form the framing scope for this book; namely, security, availability, performance, agility, and cost-effectiveness.

I have also provided useful definitions, a brief practical background on IoT and a guiding chapter on solution architecture development. The content simplified and is mainly practical; hence, it can be applied or be a supplemental input to the architectural projects at hand.

Audience

The intended audience for this book comprises information technology architects starting to produce IoT solutions, enterprise architects who want to understand the IoT solution development in large organisations and other IT professionals who wish to become IoT solution architects to produce solutions in IoT ecosystems.

It is important to state that this book covers architectural breadth rather than specialist level depth for IoT ecosystem building. There are some references to obtain those specialist level details from other sources, a myriad of other publications and programs developed in the IoT field on the market. IoT is a fast-growing field with a wealth of emerging literature from multiple angles and depth.

In this book, I have assumed that, as a solution architect, the reader is aware of architectural frameworks and has experience in business, data, application and technical architecture. For example, a knowledge of TOGAF (The Open Group Architecture Framework) can be beneficial, but it is not essential. I highly recommend that solution architects can articulate solutions and produce architectural models and frameworks using at least one single method. In this case, TOGAF can be a good start as it is open-source and can be learned freely. There are also commercial courses to speed up the learning of TOGAF.

In addition, this book offers a chapter on continuous learning for IoT solution architects. This book can also be a guiding reference to the CTOs (Chief Technology Officers), CDO (Chief Digital Officers), CIOs (Chief Information Officers), Head of Technology responsible for IoT ecosystems end to end.

Chapter 2 - Introduction

Importance of IoT

IoT is gaining attention and is vital because IoT technology and solutions change the things we perceive and experience in our homes, at workplaces, and in all walks of life. IoT solutions transform our environments to new levels by introducing novel frameworks and new functionalities that can have a profound impact on our lives.

This new technology and its integrated solutions allow the physical and virtual devices to have multiple human-like senses, such as hearing, seeing, thinking, and most interestingly, making decisions on behalf of human beings. This is a non-trivial situation and a fact that may concern each individual and society at various levels.

We can use IoT applications in all walks of life. From the perspectives of functionality and usability, IoT technology and its integrated solutions could save our lives, improve the quality of our lives and reduce day-to-day stress.

What is novel about IoT technologies and solutions is that they allow "things," or more precisely, devices that are not computers, to act intelligently and make collaborative decisions that are beneficial to many applications in various domains.

To further emphasise this point, IoT solutions allow things to hear, see, think or act by allowing them to communicate and coordinate with others to make logical decisions.

In short, IoT marks a paradigm shift in information technology. This shift, which allows the things to talk to each other, create services and make day-to-day decisions programmable by human beings, is an inevitable part of our lives at home, at work and almost anywhere we go.

Solution Approach and Context

In this book, I provide a practical approach based on solid architectural principles and industry trends. I based this book on my experience and professional thought leadership process. I am a lead Enterprise Solution Architect with over 20 years' experience and have been in the IT industry for over 35 years.

Even though I have an academic background at the doctoral level, in this book, I have only reflected upon my industry experience, and thus, chose not to include any academic perspectives. The reason for excluding the academic aspect is because there are so many theory-based books about IoT that rarely add any hands-on value to IoT solution architects. However, these books have different centres of interest, such as learning the theory behind the concepts and guidelines. So, to confirm, this book is not academic; instead, it is based on practical guidance.

While authoring this book, I conducted a comprehensive review of the practical industry-based literature on IoT. Through my findings, I concluded that there was a pressing need for secure, agile, highly available, well-performing, and cost-effective IoT systems. I found out that the contemporary issues in the literature and associated media mainly revolve around the five topics that comprise the critical business concerns; namely, security, availability, performance, agility and cost-effectiveness. In this book, these five key points comprise the use cases of effective and efficient IoT solutions. However, feel free to name them with whatever adjectives are suitable to describe the quality of the solutions desired by the stakeholders.

Through my experience, I found that an

enterprise architecture approach to creating an ecosystem, which considers the five major use cases covered in this book, can provide a useful framework to meet the expectations of the stakeholders for the IoT solutions. Enterprise Architecture is a comprehensive domain spanning across all aspects of information technology (IT) in organisations, and there are times that enterprise solution architects deal with intractable problems in complex IT environments.

Due to the broad scope of enterprise solution architecture, in this book, I have focused explicitly on narrow use cases that are universal to all modern IT environments and IoT ecosystems in particular. These universal use cases (security, availability, performance, agility, and cost-effectiveness) form the primary context for this book. For example, when any IT professionals or sponsoring executives responsible for IoT in their organisations are asked to comment on their expectations from IoT solutions, they would all most likely echo the following statements:

- We need secure IoT devices.
- We need these devices urgently.

- We want these devices to be available at all times.
- We need these devices to perform well.
- We want these devices to be cost-effective.

Considering these universal use cases in the form of non-functional aspects of the solutions, we need to find smart ways to create architectural solutions to accommodate these use cases in a structured, integrated and coherent manner because we know that any architectural solution requires a coherent structure. Moreover, as IoT solution architects, it is paramount that we understand the critical pain points and concerns associated with these use cases. These use cases are comprehensive and sophisticated and require specialised skills. For example, the security use case requires multiple security specialists to address the different security aspects of a solution. The same rule applies for performance, availability, agility and the financial aspects. We touch upon all these use cases at a high level to cover the architectural breadth.

In this book, I have dedicated a distinct chapter to each non-functional characteristic and by using architectural principles and industry best practices. The titles used for these use cases are as follows:

- Security Architecture for IoT
- Agile Architecture for IoT
- Availability & Performance Architecture for IoT (combined)
- Effective Cost Models for IoT

The content in this book may also provide input to lead IoT solution architects when creating a reference architecture for future IoT solutions. The guiding principles and lessons learned from the field can be valuable when establishing reference architectures that focus on performance, availability, security, agility, and cost-effectiveness. Let us now turn to discuss the importance of IoT as I wrote this book with this specific point in mind.

Defining IoT for Solution Architects

In simple terms, we can define IoT as connecting, networking, integrating, and managing things (physical devices) via the internet using embedded chips integrated with several components. Management is a large part of the IoT because it includes collecting and processing data using various processes, tools and technology stacks.

The major components of IoT solutions are software, hardware, networks, electronics, sensors and actuators. These components enable things (physical objects) to exchange data and make the data readable and easily understandable to allow architects to take in a wide variety of use cases that affect our business, social and personal lives.

From a technological perspective, we add an intelligent chip to an object. In the most straightforward format, the core component—a chip—can be explained as a kind of sensor for the intended object communicating to another object or human being. The object can obtain data and transmit the data via the internet to a data repository. Then, the data repository, which has an analytical system, transforms the data into information and knowledge. This processed information or knowledge can be understood by humans and, consequently, helps them to take the intended action.

By definition, the IoT also requires the inclusion of actuators. We can define an actuator as a mechanism for turning energy into motion. Actuators require control signals and sources of energy We can add more intelligence and functions to IoT systems by using actuators. These are the components responsible for moving or controlling the IoT systems. Based on their functions, actuators can be mechanical, electronic, hardware or software systems.

Defining IoT without a specific context can be challenging. Different professionals can define it differently based on their knowledge, skills and experience with IoT. After reading the following sections, you can gain a broader perspective of IoT solutions, especially from an architectural angle, and be equipped with the ability to create better definitions for IoT that may suit your needs.

The Big Deal for IoT

When it comes to IoT, many of us ask about what the big deal is, or whether IoT is just hype. In my view, the development of IoT has not come about through hype; the big deal surrounding IoT is the extended intelligence introduced to our lives by providing the connection of devices and the use of massive data transforming into knowledge and real-life actions.

One major use case for these real-life actions for IoT is being able to manage our cars, homes, workplaces and many devices intelligently, efficiently, securely and remotely, whenever we need them.

Substantial progress has been made in many disciplines owing to the use of IoT in creating new services and products. Some of these disciplines include environmental monitoring, manufacturing, infrastructure management, energy management, agriculture, healthcare, transportation, IT, electronics, material sciences and banking.

Another primary reason for the success of IoT is the fast-paced progress of IoT. In the market, it is noticeable that IoT technologies are emerging and IoT solutions are growing exponentially. Some organisations estimate that we may have billions of devices in the next few years. For example, Gartner points out that, by 2020, there may be nearly 20.8 billion devices on the IoT.

The bottom line is that IoT is valuable for both business and economy, which is inevitable. From our current experience, we can construe that IoT will most likely have a substantial impact on our economy and the way we do business and commerce.

Consumers and Service Providers have an incredible interest and focus on this fantastic technology powered by the internet. The generation of new business for companies and new job roles that we cannot even name yet is imminent. Some believe that the IoT can be as important as the emergence of the internet itself. Some even point out that it can be the next big thing in our lives. These are, of course, speculations, combined with some media hype; however, time can tell as to whether the high expectations of IoT can be met.

Ignoring the hype, let's briefly touch on the specific benefits and values in the next session before we delve into the architectural topics.

Benefits and Value Propositions of IoT

The main benefit and value proposition of IoT comes from collecting an enormous amount of data from various means and devices and then building services based on analyses of this massive amount of data. Building new services from such a collection of data would result in a substantial outcome with multiple implications.

IoT solutions (products and services), paradoxically, allow us to learn more about ourselves from various angles than ourselves alone. What does this statement mean? Here is a simple example taken from daily life. There are several IoT devices on the market. These devices can provide us with information on numerous health factors, such as sleep, nutrition, exercise, blood tests, and overall health.

A sophisticated smartwatch can monitor our health, alert us about risks and take appropriate actions for us. A simple Fitbit device can inform our sleep patterns as it is naturally impossible for a human being to monitor their sleep without using such a device. Hence, such devices have real value when implemented in daily life.

Another value of the IoT is that it helps us predict the future; hence, the more data provided to the IoT systems, the better the analyses and outcomes can be. These data-rich analyses help us predict the future better and intervene before any potential damage occurs.

As IoT synthesises data via cognitive analytics, IoT solutions can help us gain better insights from structured, unstructured, dynamic or static data by integrating with cognitive systems. Like humans, a cognitive system undertakes the duties of learning, understanding, planning, problem-solving, deciding, analysing, synthesising and assessing.

We can use IoT solutions in many facets of our lives to control our economies. These solutions can be used at home or in our workplaces for various reasons. For example, some IoT solutions can be used to reduce food wastage, while they can inform us when food is needed and where it is needed. Such solutions, for instance, can be implemented in the fridges in our kitchen, which connect to various other locations, such as grocery stores in an automated way.

IoT systems are expected to get smarter.

These progressive, smart devices can predict what we need and want. These devices can even construct bridges between generations. For example, they can help us create a memory repository, which can then be passed on to the next generations to preserve knowledge and shed light on their ancestral heritage. Imagine if IoT existed 5000 years ago? We could have learned so much about our ancestors, and hence, we wouldn't have made the mistakes they made.

As an extended electronic ecosystem, IoT solutions can help to eliminate cumbersome technology. For example, undesirable noise, screens and hardware clutter can shade gradually, and we only deal with the active service providers around us. In other words, technology can be supportive, rather than intrusive.

IoT solutions can use several applications. Some typical applications of IoT solutions are listed below:

- Home Entertainment
- Home automation and control such as smart lighting
- Industrial control
- Robotics
- Medical data collection
- Workplace safety and security

- Embedded sensing in buildings

  - Remote control
  - Traffic control
  - Self-driving cars

Important Points Excluded this Book

There are many questions in the online discussion forums regarding various moral aspects that may have implications on society, autonomy, safety, and security.

I am mindful not to load the readers' brains with too much philosophical and conceptual details. For example, the following questions can go into very much detail; in fact, they can take excessive pages in this book; hence we consider them out of the scope of this book.

- What sort of intelligence will IoT pose?
- Who will make critical decisions when things go wrong?
- How will paradoxes be addressed?

Although the media often discuss important philosophical factors, such as loss of human control or leaving choices to machines, and creating transformational digital twins for economic gains, these are broad topics and excluded from the scope of this book.

Even though these are valid, important and necessary points in terms of design, these aspects cannot be covered extensively in this guidance book; however, they could appear in the next edition of the book, or additional books that I can author in this field, as the technology becomes more widespread.

Chapter Summary and Key Points

The primary use cases of IoT are: We need secure IoT devices urgently; we want these devices to be available all the time; we need these devices to perform well, and we want these devices to be cost-effective.

IoT technology and solutions change the things we perceive and experience in our homes, workplaces and environments for the overall society.

IoT solutions equip physical and or virtual devices with multiple human-like senses, such as hearing, seeing and thinking, and most interestingly, making useful decisions on behalf of human beings.

IoT marked a paradigm shift in information technology.

The major components of IoT solutions are software, hardware, network, electronics, sensors and actuators.

IoT technologies are emerging, and IoT solutions are exponentially growing on the market.

IoT has a prominent potential for business and economy.

The main benefit and value proposition of IoT comes from collecting an enormous amount of data from various means and devices and then building services upon the analysis of these massive data.

IoT solutions can help us gain more insight from structured, unstructured, dynamic or static data by integrating with cognitive systems.

As an electronic ecosystem, IoT can assist in making cumbersome technology disappear.

There are many applications for IoT, such as home entertainment, home automation, industrial control, medical data collection, and remote control.

Chapter 3: Context and Components of IoT Ecosystem

The IoT Context

Before we look at the IoT Solution Architecture in detail, we first need to understand the context and the components of the IoT ecosystem. Understanding the context can help us delve into architecture and design topics.

From a contextual perspective, IoT solutions include several factors. The key factors are the Things (devices), Gateways, the Internet, Communications, Processes, Tools, and Users. A combination of the Things and the Internet include wireless technologies, microcontrollers and services. The Internet connects these devices to enable them to communicate with each other to exchange data and information.

IoT devices can have multiple roles. For example, we can plan the devices as either a source or a destination for the data and information in the network. Interestingly, some devices can be the source, destination or both at the same time.

The most prominent part of IoT systems is

the control mechanism since they can be simultaneously a controller or be controlled, with the ultimate goal being that the system takes action and produces the desired results. In other words, a device can control other devices, and it can be controlled by other devices in the network. The reason for emphasising this point is that these two-way control-based interactions create an enormous challenge for security, performance, availability and cost.

We can store the IoT-related data in sensors, gateways, local devices in the network and the Cloud at different amounts. For example, sensors may hold very little (bare minimum data) while a Cloud-based storage device may hold terabytes of data for analysis and data visualisation. Gateways and Edge servers also store a certain amount of data to provide necessary calculations that improve the performance and availability requirements of a system.

Based on several well-known performance and availability challenges, it is clear that the IoT control mechanisms need to be well understood, well-structured and designed in the most granular way possible to ensure the interactions are based on the intended security objectives. Of course, we also need to add agility to this context.

A methodical architectural approach is

essential to overcome these challenges and produce the desired results. To produce and support these devices on an ongoing basis, we keep these control mechanisms highly available, well-performing, and cost-effective.

Now, let's look at the IoT ecosystem and understand the key players in this complex and dynamic environment.

The IoT Ecosystem Players

A typical IoT ecosystem is made of simple or complex multiple systems, components, sub-components, integrated, single-tasking or multitasking elements. Since these components and elements need to work coherently and in harmony; therefore, the environment is called the ecosystem.

This book proposes a new architectural approach to the IoT ecosystem. To be able to create sustainable architectures and designs, it is essential to create and understand the ecosystem, its components and its mechanism. In addition, the approach factors in the survival mechanisms and its integration requirements for extending or enhancing the electronic ecosystem cause it to resemble a biological ecosystem.

This new perspective includes a strong, agile architectural focus on IoT solutions without compromising the quality of architectural deliverables, such as security, privacy, performance, availability and cost-effectiveness.

In the following sections, we cover the key players involved in a high-level IoT ecosystem.

Things of IoT

The crucial first player of the IoT regards the 'things', which are intelligent hardware devices, such as sensors and actuators. IoT devices require microcontrollers and microprocessors with a chipset to enable wireless connections and communications. These chipsets can be made up of some commercially available boards that we can use for prototyping a solution component.

IoT hardware boards typically include components, such as a battery, power supply, reset button, on/off button, LEDs, gyroscope, Wi-Fi, USB interface, Camera, I2C Connector, Ethernet connector, Micro HDMI connector, and an LVDS display.

There are numerous prototyping boards available on the market. They are inexpensive and can speed up the prototyping process considerably to develop a quick IoT solution. Some popular boards are Intel Edison, Arduino, BeagleBone, UDOO Neo Photon, RaspberryPi, and ESP8266.

IoT End-Users

IoT end-users are usually remote to the Things or the technical backend systems. In some cases, user can be part of them or close to them. These end-users are also known as consumers from a service management perspective. In general, these end-users do not have direct access to or have a view of the back-end systems.

The users send commands (from their input devices) via the Internet to the analytics servers. It is challenging to set the proximity for the end-users unless we know the use cases for the applications they use.

For example, for an application sensing a user's heart rate and sleep patterns, the user generally carries the device on their arms. In this case, the proximity is close, almost embedded. However, if they obtain information about the weather conditions on a remote farm, they can view this information on a smartphone, even if the farm is kilometres away.

IoT Gateways

The IoT Gateways are the raw data processing and transmission devices. These gateways are the communication points between sensors and the Cloud. Data coming from the sensors pass through the Gateways to reach to the Cloud.

In the IoT technical literature, and particularly in architectural documents, IoT gateways are also known as 'control tiers'. These devices can be implemented as hardware or software solutions.

The primary purpose of these gateways is to minimise the high volume of data generated by the sensors. Some IoT gateways have additional intelligence for analysing data and only send the relevant data to the Cloud storage units.

Some IoT gateways also provide additional security mechanisms, such as adding encrypted transmissions. Architects need to pay special attention to these devices and factor in the performance, availability, security and cost-effectiveness criteria in their solutions.

Considering smarter gateways in IoT solutions is vital in terms of data performance. These gateways can perform tasks such as averaging data and making more effective calculations, even before the data sets are transferred to the analytics servers.

Gateways can connect to the Internet directly or via edge devices. However, as an architectural principle, processing raw data should be performed by the edge devices to improve performance efficiency, and in particular, prevent network latency and data transmission delays in the ecosystem.

It can be useful to make an architectural decision in the solution document to find out why the Internet can sometimes be either directly accessed by the gateway or only through the edge device.

There can be specific considerations for each use case, and they need to be articulated in the solution document as an architectural decision. Determining such a decision upfront and obtain consensus on these decisions can yield many benefits when the solution goes to production support.

IoT Cloud

We all know the recent trends for Cloud Computing. Cloud marked a paradigm shift to Information Technology and Computing field. IoT Cloud is a critical player in the ecosystem. The central role the Cloud plays in IoT is to facilitate the data integration of the solution components effectively.

IoT solutions are mainly used to provide real-time information to consumers. The data required to generate real-time information can be massive in scale. The Cloud, along with computing power, storage, networking, analytics, metering, billing, and other service management components, can make this information available for the consumers.

The integration of Cloud to IoT can create new revenue streams. Integrating the Cloud with the IoT can create new business models enriched by real-time analysis and directly consumed information at the same time. In other words, without the Cloud, the IoT can hardly add any value due to its real-time data and information-rich nature.

The addition of the Cloud to the IoT can also contribute to improved security, availability and performance of the IoT solutions. Cloud providers have rigorous security, availability and performance metrics established based on a service consumption model. In particular, IoT-enabled Cloud systems seem to pose additional security measures.

When integrated with Edge computing, Cloud computing can add better value to the IoT ecosystem. The main reason for this is that Edge computing can do the filtering for the Cloud to focus on the usable data.

Therefore, the IoT solution architects need to understand the Cloud Computing architecture and service models and how to integrate them into the IoT solutions. Being aware of the capabilities of Cloud technologies and using them effectively in the solution work products can be beneficial in creating large-scale commercial IoT solutions.

IoT Platforms

IoT platforms play a unique and essential role in an IoT ecosystem. IoT platforms consist of multi-layer technology stacks that enable automatic provisioning, system management, and overall automation of connected devices in the ecosystem.

Some IoT platforms aim to fill the space that exists between sensors and networks. Specific platforms can connect the sensors and the network using specifically developed functions or applications.

There are many platforms commercially available on the market. It can be useful for IoT solution architects to familiarise themselves with the offering services of these popular platforms. We can use some of these products in an integrated way in an IoT ecosystem. I provide a list of popular web-based platforms. The list is in alphabetical order to make it easier to remember.

- Ayla Network IoT
- Amazon Web Services IoT
- ARMmbed IoT Device
- Artik IoT
- Bosch IoT Suite

- Carriots PaaS
- Cisco IoT Cloud Connect
- General Electric's Predix
- Google Cloud Platform
- HP Universal of Things
- IBM Watson IoT Platform
- Kaa IoT Platform
- LTI Mosaic Things
- Microsoft Azure IoT Platform
- Mindsphere by Siemens
- Mocana Full-Stack
- Oracle Integrated Cloud
- Salesforce IoT Cloud
- Thingspeak IoT Platform
- ThingWorx IoT Platform

IoT Systems Layout

From an architectural point of view, in IoT systems, embedded objects need to be aligned with the environment. Each object is an essential member of the ecosystem. Therefore, we need to design them with an integrated approach. These objects must work in harmony and must be enabled through a well-architected, well-designed and coherent approach.

From the perspective of usability, the IoT

system layout needs to be simple. Solution architects need to make specific considerations with regards to the layout. For example, we need to ensure that the layout is not cluttered with a myriad of cables and disturbing hardware components. Modern consumers hate clutter and disturbing objects in their devices. Besides simplicity is desirable and can be considered an enabling factor for security, performance, availability and cost.

The simplicity provided in terms of usability can have a favourable effect on users' senses and prevent any potential damage to their health. This usability factor also can be part of the non-functional requirements (NFRs) and traced to the building blocks of the solution outcomes.

IoT Hardware

IoT hardware components are an essential aspect of the overall IoT ecosystem. We can categorise IoT hardware over the following points, and use cases briefly explained under each section below.

The Things of IoT

We mention the things once more here. The reason to repeat the things here is to provide an architectural perspective when discussing the ecosystem. The Things are the most foundational aspect of the IoT solutions.

To recap, the 'Things' in IoT are the sensor devices. They are usually physical sensors embedded in or on objects to sense various physical activities such as sound, light, speed, and velocity. Things can be either battery-powered or energy harvested and can have embedded code or embedded operating systems.

We can categorise IoT devices under three main topics. The first one concerns the smallest devices with embedded 8-bit systems, which are also known as System on Chips (SOCs) devices. SoCs have given rise to many commercial devices. Some SoCs can run full operating systems and calculate complex algorithms.

The second ones are the 32-bit systems based on Atheros or ARM Chips which run a cut-down version of open-source operating systems such as Linux, while the third ones are the 64-bit computing platforms running full versions of operating systems such as Linux, Windows or Android.

The 'Things' can function as converters or talk to a separate device that plays the role of an additional converter. The function of these 'Things' is to convert the physical signals to digital signals.

Edge Devices

Edge Computing is a crucial architectural factor in IoT. Edge devices can have multiple functions in the IoT ecosystem. These devices are instrumental and contribute to performance, availability and security goals in IoT solutions. Edge devices are useful when integrated with Cloud systems. We can connect Gateways to the edge devices.

Edge devices play several roles, such as to process data, reduce the amount of data and optimise data for better communication on the internet. Edge devices can process and upload the data to the Internet (preferably to a Cloud system) via the TCP/IP; that is, the significant and native protocol of the Internet.

Using Edge Computing architecture, we can ensure that an application can process sensitive data on-site. Then, the application, for further analysis, can only send the privacy-compliant data to the Cloud. Edge computing has a favourable impact on IoT security and privacy solutions.

There is an important architecture related to Edge Computing that IoT solution architects need to know—Fog Computing or Fog Networking. Fog Computing architecture uses Edge devices to maintain a large amount of computation, storage and communication processes locally and then route them over the Internet. The critical strength of Fog computing is its proximity to consumers. This proximity can constitute enormous performance implications in the solutions.

For IoT solution architects, it is fundamental to understand Fog Computing architecture as it has a favourable impact on the availability and performance of IoT solutions, primarily via a reduction in latency and by improving quality of services in networking terms.

IoT Storage

In IoT solutions, storage devices can be placed either in the Edge or in the Cloud. Due to performance considerations, the storage function can usually be performed by the Edge devices, as mentioned in the previous section.

Our IoT solution may need several architectural decisions as far as IoT storage is concerned. For example, we can make an architectural decision on whether to have additional storage devices at the backend before the data is sent to the Cloud. Other architectural decisions can be related to a high ratio of storage capacity to the physical footprint, speed, reliability and data security.

IoT Analytics Computation

We use IoT analytics to make sense of massive data; for example depicting key performance indicators in the visualisation application in a dashboard. These dashboards can include risk management views, errors, bottlenecks and view things in real-time.

IoT solutions need computers to perform analytics and intelligence activities. Such tasks are hosted by Cloud platforms, such as analytics applications in which computation performance is important. We also need to consider storage. For analytics storage, we need to make an architectural decision as to whether local storage or cloud-based storage is better. This architectural decision is necessary to address cost and performance concerns.

IoT Analytics can also be provided as a consumption-based service. For example, AWS IoT Analytics is a fully managed IoT analytics service that collects, pre-processes, enriches, stores and analyses IoT device data. AWS customers can also bring their own custom analysis packaged in a container to execute AWS IoT Analytics.

End-user Devices and Communication

End-user devices are sensors that are used

to communicate with end-users, systems or platforms. There is a growing amount of research on direct end-user interaction with and via IoT devices. The interactions are usually accomplished via a wide variety of smartphones, tablets and laptop machines connected to the Internet.

For example, some users can access their home automation devices, such as security cameras, remotely via their smartphones and interact with the home automation systems at their convenience when they are away from home.

There are also other popular user devices, such as wearable fitness watches. These watches collect the data from human body motions and send them to the analytics machines in the Cloud, which could be hosted any part of the globe.

Prototyping Boards

Prototyping boards can be very useful and cost-effective when employed to analyse availability and performance concerns in an agile way. Prototyping is the process of building IoT systems enhanced with sensors and embedded systems using off-the-shelf components. Many inexpensive off-the-shelf components, such as microcontrollers, sensors and circuit boards, are available in the market for consumption.

IoT prototyping boards are microcontrollers or microprocessors with chipsets to handle wireless connections. These development boards, when used with the IoT Cloud platform, enable a fast prototyping process.

APIs for IoT

APIs (Application Programming Interfaces) are part of the IoT ecosystem to allow secure connections to the consumers, channels and other IoT applications. We can use APIs to integrate devices, applications, data, and Cloud systems quickly and effectively.

Further, APIs can contribute to the performance, availability and security goals. APIs also help the production of solutions in an agile and cost-effective manner. Considering APIs cover the main architectural objectives mentioned in this book, they are highly recommended to be understood and included in the IoT solution process.

Overall, APIs can be compelling components of the IoT ecosystem when we use them correctly in our solutions. APIs can provide fast and effective automation. We know that we can reduce any human errors and increase the speed of throughput using automation

IoT Standards

Due to the complexity and comprehensiveness of IoT, we certainly need standards in place for developing solutions. IoT solutions require new standard devices, protocols and communication mechanisms. There are several standards developed by various organisations. Therefore, it is essential to understand the IoT standards offered by IEEE, IETF and ITU. Some of the established IoT standards are:

- IoT Data Link Standards
- IoT MAC Standards
- IoT Routing Standards
- IoT Network Standards
- IoT Transport Layer Standards
- IoT Management Standards

There are additional IoT standards developed by Open-source designers, such as The Open Group. The IoT work-group has, thus far, produced two Open Group IoT standards for the IoT lifecycle management. These lifecycle management standards are called O-DF (Open Data Format) and the O-MI (Open Messaging Interface).

Another large organisation providing IoT

standards is the LoRa Alliance, which is a non-profit association of more than 500-member companies. The organisation claims that,

> The LoRa Alliance is committed to enabling large scale deployment of Low Power Wide Area Networks (LPWAN) IoT through the development and promotion of the LoRaWAN open standard. Members benefit from a vibrant ecosystem of active contributors offering solutions, products and services, which create new and sustainable business opportunities. Through standardisation and the accredited certification scheme, the LoRa Alliance delivers the interoperability needed for LPWA networks to scale, making LoRaWAN the premier solution for global LPWAN deployments.

There are also other organisations, such as The Things Network, which provide a set of open tools and a global, open network to build maximum security and ready to scale IoT applications at low cost.

IoT Standard Protocols

IoT solutions require several standard protocols and newly developed IoT specific protocols. While designing IoT protocols, we need to consider long-range communication systems and protocols such as LPWAN (low-power wide-area network). LPWAN is a kind of wireless protocol operating at a low bit rate. LPWAN enables long-range communications between connected IoT devices to a Cloud system via wireless gateways.

LPWAN is known to have low energy requirements. On the IoT market, you may hear a lot about LoRaWAN deployments. IT is an LPWAN protocol that connects IoT devices using LoRa Wireless Technology. LoRa can be used for both public and private deployments and runs on unlicensed frequencies worldwide. LoRa enables a long battery life for devices in IoT ecosystems. LoRaWAN can be extended up to 30 km in flat areas.

Another protocol worth mentioning related to IoT is Sigfox, which uses UNB (Ultra NarrowBand). Sigfox signals have better spectral efficiency and can reduce any potential noise. Another vital benefit of Sigfox is that it offers a longer battery life, which, consequently, may have a positive impact on cost. Sigfox is a global company that is based in France. Their assertion certainly needs to be considered from the perspectives of cost-effectiveness, performance and availability. Here is a quote from their technology website:

Sigfox is rolling out the first global IoT network to listen to billions of objects broadcasting data, without the need to establish and maintain network connections. This unique approach in the world of wireless connectivity, where there is no signalling overhead, a compact and optimised protocol, and where objects are not attached to the network. Sigfox offers a software-based communications solution, where all the network and computing complexity is managed in the Cloud, rather than on devices. All that together, it drastically reduces energy consumption and costs of connected devices.

In the near future, the launch of 5G connectivity can show real promise. 5G is the fifth generation of cellular wireless protocol. At present, most IoT implementations use 4G, which is insufficient when dealing with large volumes of data generated by a large number of IoT devices. Therefore, there is a growing focus on 5G as a promising enabler of futuristic IoT capabilities. Experts believe that 5G can create more IoT-friendly ecosystems. Some of the significant benefits of 5G are that it can speed up data transmission and reduce latency dramatically. In addition, the introduction of 5G could bring a 90% reduction in network energy usage.

There are also Edge and Cloud Computing protocols, especially Middleware-related protocols that need to be considered for various use cases. Some important ones to consider are STOMP (Simple Text Oriented Messaging Protocol), MQTT (MQ Telemetry Transport), CoAP (Constrained Application Protocol) and AMQP (Advanced Message Queuing Protocol). While STOMP, MQTT and CoAP focus on increasing availability and performance for resource-poor environments, AMQP is more focused on increasing security.

The table below contains a list of the most popular protocols used in IoT solutions based on a broad category with examples. As IoT solution architects, knowing the pros and cons of these protocols can be highly beneficial as this knowledge can help architects make better decisions as far as IoT protocols are concerned.

Category	Protocol Examples
Discovery	mDNS, DNS-SD
Session Layer	HTTP, MQTT, COAP, AMQP, XMPP
Communications and Transport	Bluetooth, LPWAN, Wifi
Identification	uCode, IPv6, URIs, EPC,
Network Layer	6LoWPAN, 6TiSCH, 6Lo, IPv6 over G.9959, IPv6 over Bluetooth Low Energy, RPL, CORPL, CARP
Data Link Layer	Zigbee Smart Energy, Sigfox, LTE-A, LoRaWAN, WirelessHART, Z-Wave, Bluetooth Low Energy, DASH7, HomePlug, G.9959,

	Weightless, DECT/ULE, IEEE 802.15.4e, IEEE 802.11 ah
Device Management	TR-069, OMA-DM
Semantic	JSON-LD, IOTDB
Multi-layer Frameworks	Alljoyn, IoTivity, Weave, Homekit

IoT Applications

Many applications form a part of the IoT ecosystem. These applications can offer various use cases for different consumer types. Some common IoT Application types are smart homes, wearables, smart cities, smart grids, industrial internet, connected cars, connected health, smart retail, smart supply chain and smart farming.

Our solution architecture may need to implement one or more of these applications in an integrated way. As IoT solution architects, we may also design solutions for new IoT applications rather than using commercially available applications.

To start with, understanding the business requirements and use cases can help you to choose an application or make an architectural decision to create an in-house IoT application. You can also obtain use case ideas from IoTONE that offer 54 high-level use cases, such as Building Energy Management Systems, Continuous Emission Monitoring Systems, Fleet

Management, Indoor Air Quality Monitoring, and the Last Mile Delivery. You can review these famous use cases by IoTONE from the link provided in Appendix B.

To learn more about various IoT applications and relevant IoT technologies in the industry, you can review the top 500 Industrial IoT companies as listed by IoTOne. See the link provided in Appendix B. The list provides information on each IoT company.

IoT Communication Patterns

It can be useful for architects to be familiar with IoT communication patterns. They can simplify the solution progress by providing established resolutions to a communication problem. These patterns can be categorised based on their functions under the names of Information Flows, Queries, Commands and Notifications. I have given a brief explanation of the flow in the following list:

1. Information Flows depict the information going through the devices and the systems carrying out the status of the device or the system.
2. Queries are for requests to initiate communication activities.

3. Commands are the instructions used to perform specific communication activities.
4. Notifications depict changes in status.

Several communication patterns can be used for IoT Solutions. We need to understand the content of a pattern that may suit a specific IoT communication solution building block. We do not go into the details of each pattern here; however, it can be useful to at least be aware of the names of the commonly used communication patterns in IoT solutions which can be obtained from various reference sources in the IoT literature.

- Request and Response
- Event Subscription
- Asynchronous Messaging
- Reliable Messaging
- Multicasting
- Publish and Subscribe
- Queues
- Message Brokers
- Federation
- Discovery
- Delegation of Trust

Chapter Summary and Take Away Points

IoT solutions include Things (devices), Gateways, the internet, Communications and Users.

The IoT data can be stored in sensors, gateways, local devices in the network and the Cloud in varying amounts.

The IoT ecosystem is made of either simple or complex multiple systems, components, sub-components, integrated, single-tasking or multitasking elements.

IoT gateways are communication points between sensors and the Cloud. Data coming from the sensors pass through the Gateways to reach the Cloud.

IoT gateways can minimise the high volume of data generated by the sensors.

IoT gateways can provide additional security mechanisms (e.g., encrypted transmissions).

Processing data should be performed by the edge devices for efficiency.

IoT Cloud facilitates the data integration of the systems.

IoT Cloud can improve the security, availability and performance of IoT systems.

Edge computing can do the filtering for the Cloud to focus on the real data.

IoT platforms connect the sensors and the network using specifically developed functions or applications.

From a usability perspective, the IoT system layout needs to be simple.

The Things in IoT are the sensor devices.

We can use APIs to integrate devices, applications, data and the cloud systems quickly and effectively.

There are several standards developed by various organisations, such as IEEE, IETF and ITU.

IoT solutions require several standard protocols and newly developed IoT specific protocols.

Some typical IoT Applications are smart homes, wearables, smart cities, smart grids, industrial internet, connected cars, connected health, smart retail, smart supply chain and smart farming.

IoT communication patterns are useful to speed up the solution process. They can be categorised under the following names: Information Flows, Queries, Commands, Notifications. It can be useful to find the right pattern for a specific solution building block.

Chapter 4: A Practical Guide for IoT Architectural Solutions

Purpose

In this chapter, I provide an overview of the Solution Architecture process. We can have a high-level walkthrough of the critical architectural tasks for creating an IoT solution. As IoT solutions can include a wide variety of applications, functions and other solution elements, we cover them under an umbrella term of 'IoT Solutions'. You can customise the approach provided in this chapter to your projects at hand.

An Overview of a Solution Architecture

Let me introduce the essential architectural tasks required to create a solution at a high level. We name these architectural tasks 'solution work-products'. Open source or proprietary architectural methods also call these tasks 'work-products'. A work-product is a solution template and is an industry term in the architectural speak.

Solution architects create or deal with multiple architectural work-products. These work-products are template documents that prompt the solution architects to enter the required information with guiding notes. Work-product templates are created based on experience and lessons learned from previous successful projects. There can be many work-products for a specified solution.

There can be hundreds of work-products in sophisticated solution methods. As this book aims to provide architectural guidance and information on a few specific themes, we do not go into details of each work-product; instead, we can only focus on the main work-products related to our scope. You can obtain the details on various work-products through the use of an architectural method, such as TOGAF or Zachman. There are also many publications on architecture development and solution design methods. Therefore, this section is kept brief to ensure the context is clear and concise.

Let's briefly touch on the key points to show the context for the architectural approach. Architecture starts with thinking; in fact, with strategic thinking. As solution architects, we ask lots and lots of questions. One of the critical questions we ask is where we are now, where we are going as our target, and how to go there. This approach implies understanding the current environment, setting up the future environment, and creating a method and relevant mechanisms to move from the current sate to the future state. This is the most fundamental task of a high-level solution architect.

Architectural thinking is a process reflected by the day-to-day activities of the solution architects. This type of thinking is also facilitated by following an established method which serves the purpose of a map for the target solution architecture. Architectural thinking also considers the functional and non-functional aspects of the solution.

Architectural thinking is an essential skill for any architect. Like methodical practitioners, solution architects start working on a brief by first understanding the requirements set by the client. Therefore, requirements analysis is a fundamental architectural activity.

Solution architects create technical requirements based on business requirements. It is common for solution architects only to review the technical requirements created by technical and operational specialists and consider their solutions.

A requirements analysis may take up to several days to weeks or months, depending on the complexity of the projects at hand. The requirements are put in a matrix and analysed systematically to ensure nothing falls into the cracks.

A structured approach to a requirements analysis helps architects to understand mandatory and optional requirements and how they are met with adequate justification. For this approach, we use a requirements traceability matrix. This matrix helps us to track the requirements once the solution is drafted. The requirements traceability process continues until the successful completion of the solution.

The requirements need to be reviewed, endorsed and approved by various stakeholders. Once the requirements are approved by a governance body in the organisation, the solution architects can then start other architectural activities, such as setting the System Context.

Based on understanding the requirements, the context (preferably presented as a diagram) can be used to show the entities and relationships of the solution components at the highest level.

The System Context helps the key stakeholders understand the solution as an end-to-end service or a system. The System Context is usually represented on a single page. It is an ideal communication tool for senior executives and business stakeholders to see the bigger picture of the solution.

The System Context is also beneficial for technical team members, project managers and any other stakeholders working on the solution. Let's keep in mind that the System Context rarely changes once it is understood and approved.

Solution architects document, review and analyse the current environment. The Current Environment work-product includes the details of the hardware, software, operating systems, functionalities, service levels, operational status, and so on. This document can be very detailed. It can also have a master document linking various aspects of the current systems. Without understanding the current system, it is not feasible to define the future system.

Based on the context and requirements, the solution architects set the future environment. This future environment is also called the target environment in architectural vernacular. The target environment requires substantial foundational architectural thinking. Requirements must be crystal clear when defining the future environment. A comprehensive breadth of knowledge is essential for a solution architects to define the future state. To successfully define the future environment, solution architects need to consult subject matter experts (SMEs) to validate the solution building blocks mapped to specific requirements.

It is important to note that, in some instances, solution architects also create a transitional environment which may take place between the current and target environments. We may need this supplementary environment when we are producing a migration solution in the IoT ecosystem.

Based on the context, it can be instrumental in creating a few essential architectural models. One of the most useful models is a Component Model for the solution. A component model can start at a high level and drill down to the specific components, subcomponents and even elements of the central system. Component Models can also be useful for other stakeholders in a technical and business capacity to understand the components of the system and the relationships between them.

Solution architects also create another useful work-product—the operational model, which can be both logical and physical. The operational model shows how the solution can operate before we implement it. This work-product can be used to gain the confidence of financial sponsors and other key project stakeholders. The operational model work-product brings everyone onto the same page in terms of how the system can operate.

In addition to the Component and Operational Models, there may be other models that solution architects need to develop. Some of the other critical architectural models are the performance model, availability model, business continuity model, configuration model and the deployment model.

In addition to the architectural models, every Solution Architect needs to create and maintain the Solution Viability. The Solution Viability work-product includes the major architectural and technical issues, risks, dependencies and assumptions.

Project managers usually conduct the project or overall program Viability Assessments. The Solution Architect needs to develop and maintain the architectural and technical Viability Assessments.

Viability Assessment work-product remains dynamic throughout the solution development lifecycle. However, it is not only simple assessment tool; we can also use it as a powerful communication tool for the relevant stakeholders of the solution who are interested in assessing the risks, issues and dependencies that might affect the solution.

Decisions are critical to solution architecture. They can have substantial implications for the success or failure of the solution. Some implications can be cost-related, while others can relate to performance, availability, security and scalability.

Solution architects need to document architectural decisions upfront. These documented decisions must be approved by a governance body in the organisation.

For micro-level designs, solution architects also need to document the design decisions and obtain approval at the program level. Design decisions usually have fewer implications than architectural decisions. However, design decisions are also important.

Depending on the size, nature and complexity of the project, solution architects can use many more architectural and design work-products. The details of all architectural work-products are beyond the scope of this book. For those who are new to the architectural field, more can be learned about work-products by following an established method such as TOGAF (The Open Group Architecture Framework).

There are also books about architectural methods focusing on creating and using work-products. For beginners, there are also industry-based architectural courses that are both online and classroom-based. These courses can help architects acquire architectural skills and knowledge about work-products.

Large organisations usually have their proprietary methods. These methods can help architects identify architectural work-products as either mandatory or desirable. Solution architects can also customise the method by selecting both mandatory and optional work-products. It is fundamental to follow an established method to create a successful solution architectures.

Architectural Domains for IoT Solutions

The field of Solution Architecture for IoT ecosystems covers a broad range of architectural domains, such as application, information, data, security, integration, infrastructure, technology, and so on. Typical IoT solutions touch almost all aspects of the architectural domain.

There is usually a lead IoT Solution Architect responsible for providing the end-to-end solution. Underneath this person's leadership are several positions; namely, the IoT Application Architect, IoT Data/Information Architect, IoT Security Architect, IoT Network Architect, IoT Infrastructure Architect and the IoT Storage Architect, among others.

The lead IoT Solution Architect is required to provide input and guidance to all the other architects. Some Lead IoT solution architects can be hands-on and create some work-products. However, in large and complex projects, the lead architects usually steer the solution progress and provide guidance and advice. In complex projects, the role of the IoT Solution Architect can be compared to that of a conductor of a symphony orchestra. In fact, in some organisations, the role is called Chief IoT

Architect.

Lead IoT solution architects provide a top-down approach to the overall solution process and the development of architecture documents. They set the solution strategy and start with other aspects of the solution hierarchically, from top to bottom. The following section defines some of the critical tasks in this top-down process.

Methodical Approach for IoT Solutions

IoT solution architects need to start the solution process through the use of a methodical approach; principally, because architecture is all about structure. Using a methodical approach, we can develop our solutions in a systematic and structured manner. The benefit of using an architectural method is that it can guide us toward what steps to take, in what order to take them and how to perform the required tasks.

To create IoT solution architectures, rather than re-inventing the wheel, we must follow an established method. Following an established method allows IoT solution architects to achieve predictable and repeatable results. These methods have evolved through their multiple uses. In turn, the techniques behind these methods have also evolved through the reuse of successful implementations, as well as the lessons learnt from failed projects.

Organisations that provide IT solutions may have their proprietary methods. Some organisations adopt industry-based standard architectural methods, such as Zachman, or open-source methods such as TOGAF, while others mix the well-established methods and develop a unique solution pathway for the solutions teams.

Each method has its work-products, and although they may use different names, the outcome generally remains the same. Based on my experience in using various methods, the most common architectural work-product names are Requirements Matrix, Use Cases, Architectural Decisions, Solution Viability, System Context, Definitions, Models such as Component and Operational Models and Deployment Roadmap, among others.

The method we choose usually prompts us to start with a strategy in mind. The following section provides an overview of the architectural strategy.

Architectural Strategy for IoT Solution

The architectural strategy takes place at the beginning of an IoT solution. Strategies help the solution team to understand where they are now and where they are going. With this strategic approach in mind, an established method can help us reach our destination most effectively. This means that setting the strategy and following the method are two vital tasks in the earlier phase of IoT solutions.

More specifically, IoT solution architects need to create an architectural strategy document, which is also called a solution strategy. The solution strategy needs to be documented by the lead IoT solution architect. We must share the solution strategy document with the key stakeholders and obtain necessary approvals from them.

The solution strategy process provides an objective assessment of the current situation. It aligns project goals with the organisational goals and ensures that all gaps are covered. The solution strategy document also documents the opportunities, threats, strengths and weaknesses of the project from the technical, commercial and financial angles.

We know that the strategy of a solution hardly changes in the later phases of the solution process. Therefore, it must be understood and approved at earlier phases. However, we can make our strategy flexible by creating changeable tactics to empower our solution strategy. These tactics can also be documented and approved as part of the solution architecture approval process.

IoT Solution Requirements

Once the strategy is set, documented and approved, the IoT lead solution architect usually starts the requirements management process. The lead architect can delegate the requirements analysis for each domain to the allocated IoT solution architects. This is because requirements for IoT applications may be different than the requirements for the infrastructure domain. However, in a smaller size project, the Lead IoT Solution Architect undertakes the requirements analysis for all IoT domains.

When analysing the IoT solution requirements, the domain architects need to look at the relevant components of the ecosystem in their domain. We have included a chapter in this book providing information on the components of a typical high-level IoT ecosystem.

Once the requirements are analysed, each requirement needs to be validated by the relevant users, sponsors and other associated stakeholders. The requirements validation process may take a considerable amount of time, based on the number of requirements. Some requirements can be comprehensive and may be difficult to validate easily. Therefore, it can be useful to sort these requirements into smaller groups.

IoT requirements need to be extra

SMART—an acronym we use to describe the quality of documents. Using the SMART acronym, we can confirm that the requirements must be specific, measurable, actionable, realistic and traceable.

One crucial aspect to the requirements analyses is the use of the MoSCoW rule, as adopted from the following Agile methods: 1) must have requirements; 2) should have, if at all possible; 3) could have, but not critical; 4) will not have this time, but potentially later.

Once the IoT Solution requirements are validated as mandatory, optional or unnecessary, the IoT solution architects in each domain draft their solutions and commence the requirements' traceability activities across the IoT solution building blocks, project or initiative.

Requirement traceability is a fundamental architectural activity that requires rigour and governance. Requirement traceability has a considerable impact on the solution end product. If we fail to trace the requirements to the solution building blocks, it can be challenging to meet the required service levels, and most likely, problems can arise in the project.

Functional & Non-Functional Requirements

Lead IoT solution architects need to pay utmost attention to both the functional and non-functional aspects of solutions. To this end, they start with requirements. Typically, we can categorise requirements under two main types: Functional and Non-Functional. Both functional and non-functional components apply to the IoT ecosystem. Coupled with the non-functional aspects, architectural rigour and flexibility need to be balanced to achieve functionality.

The lead solution architects need to understand the details of both the functional and non-functional aspect of the solution well. Functional and Non-Functional requirements are like inseparable Ying and Yang. They need to be analysed and documented in an integrated manner. Let's briefly define these two types of requirements and understand their nature.

The functional requirements of a solution involve what the system offers to the consumers as functionality to be accomplished. For example, the system may offer calculations, data processing, and workflows. Functional requirements are usually related to the consumers of the solution. They describe what the consumers expect from the solution product and services.

Non-functional aspects involve how the system can accomplish these functionalities, such as performance, availability, security, reliability, scalability, usability, configuration, and so on. These are primarily technical and operational requirements. The tasks involved in the Non-Functional requirements relate to the IT support and maintenance teams.

Due to the multiple challenges surrounding the IoT ecosystem, developing a successful IoT solution is not an easy task. Regarding the IoT Non-Functional aspects, there are multiple architectural challenges. Some of these challenges related to the non-functional aspects are mobility, reliability, scalability, configuration management, availability, interoperability, security and privacy. Let's describe some of these challenges briefly so that you can consider these points when developing your IoT solution architectures.

Mobility Challenges

Mobility is a common IoT Architecture Non-Functional aspect. IoT devices need to move a lot and change their IP address and networks frequently based on their locations. For example, the routing protocols, such as RPL, must reconstruct the DODAG (Destination Oriented,

Directed Acyclic Graph) each time a node goes off the network or joins the network, which adds substantial overhead. These minute technical details, which concern mobility, may have a severe impact on solution performance, availability, security, and cost.

Another example is that a mobility task might result in a change of service providers in a mobility process. This frequent change from one provider to another provider can add another layer of complexity due to potential service interruptions, changing gateways, and emerging hidden alerts.

Related to the mobility concerns, there is even a sub-discipline of IoT, known as the Internet of Mobile Things (IoMT). Some of the IoT mobility aspects are phones and moving vehicles such as cars, ships, trains, and planes. These devices require special considerations while developing solutions. IoT solution architects need to be aware of the changes required by mobile devices and apply the relevant techniques for mobility solution architectures.

Scalability & Capacity Challenges

Scalability is a common challenge present in IoT ecosystems. One of the critical components of the ecosystem is the IoT applications. We can define scalability as the property of a system to manage demands and an increasing workload by adding resources to the system or its components. Scalability is closely related to capacity. Capacity is the maximum amount that a system can hold, contain, process or produce.

IoT Solutions certainly require comprehensive scalability and capacity plans. IoT applications integrate with and serve a myriad of devices in the ecosystem. Managing the distribution of devices across networks and the application landscape can be a complicated task. There is a need for a dynamic increase or decrease in capacity, coupled with vertical and horizontal scalability and extendibility of the solutions.

IoT applications need to be tolerant of new services and devices joining the network at a fast speed. Addressing this challenge requires dynamic scalability and enormous extendibility.

To this end, IoT solution architects need to consider the scalability of devices, gateways, edge servers, cloud computing processes, storage capacity, the analytics process and applications. To perform Scalability and Capacity plans, we need to consider all aspects and components of the IoT ecosystem.

Scalability and capacity requirements need to be documented in the non-functional requirements document and matched to the solution building blocks. We need to be mindful that these requirements must be traceable in an IoT solution building block. A solution building block is the smallest unit of the solution from functionality perspectives.

We also need to be mindful that non-scalable or incapacitated IoT solutions may cause bottlenecks in services, create non-compliance for service level agreements, and ultimately, cause the solutions to fail and financial loss for the funding organisation.

Interoperability Challenges

Interoperability means that heterogeneous devices, solution components, elements and protocols need to be able to work with each other harmoniously. Maintaining the interoperability in an IoT ecosystem is another challenge owing to the wealth of platforms, solution components, devices and protocols used in IoT ecosystems.

Interoperability can be handled by both the application developers and the device manufacturers to deliver the services regardless of the platform or hardware specification used by the customer. However, the IoT solution architects also need to understand the interoperability implications of their IoT solutions.

IoT solution architects need to document

the interoperability requirements in the non-functional requirements document and trace them to the solution building blocks. They also need to document interoperability concerns, issues, risks and dependencies in the Solution Viability work-product.

IoT Connectivity

IoT cannot exist without connections, which, for IoT systems, is a fundamental requirement for IoT solutions. The Internet is the primary enabler of connectivity, which is often taken granted as an apparent line item. Simply put, connectivity is so fundamental that if there is no Internet, there is no IoT! For IoT solutions, use of the Internet can resemble the use of electricity when we are using an electronic device, such as a TV or radio. No electricity, no TV!

Several considerations also need to be made when it comes to internet connectivity. Some of the considerations can be the type of Internet services, Internet service providers, usage cost, communication speed and so on. Let's remember from the mobility section that mobile devices, such as moving vehicles, require unique Internet connections, such as multi-service providers based on their current locations. For example, a device moving in Europe may require internet connectivity from a

French Internet Service Provider when it is in France and from a German Internet Service Provider when it is in Germany.

Importance of Architectural Decisions for IoT Solutions

As an IoT ecosystem is sophisticated, comprehensive, and interrelated with many moving parts needed in the solution, IoT Lead Solution Architect and other domain architects need to understand all relationships. Due to this complexity, solutions can generate many options and different approaches. It is the Lead IoT Solutions Architect's role to document these options and approaches to aim for the optimal outcomes for their decisions. We need to document these options and approaches in the format of architectural decisions.

An architectural decision format can include the possible options, a description of the selected option, and the rationale for the selected option with clear recommendations. We must articulate these recommendations must in a way that all stakeholders understand the impact and implications of the selected option. Architectural Decisions documents must be clear, concise, and verifiable. They are usually single-page documents.

We must pay special attention to

architectural decisions that we make for IoT solutions as each decision can have a severe impact once the solution is implemented and the consumption process has started. The impact may be on cost, performance, and many other aspects of the solution. These decisions can even determine the destiny of the project in terms of its success or failure. Let's always keep in mind that if the architecture is wrong, then everything can go wrong.

Use Cases in IoT Solutions

IoT solution architects must obtain, analyse, understand and validate the IoT solution use cases. The validated use cases can be very beneficial for requirement validation and making architectural decisions.

A use case is a specific situation in which a product or service in a solution to be used by the consumers. We develop the use cases from the users' perspective. For an IoT solution, we need to understand how the consumers are intended to be using a particular component or aspect of the solution. Usually, the functional requirements can help us to formulate the use cases; or, in some circumstances, use cases help formulate the Functional Requirements. This means that use cases and solution requirements are interrelated. We need to analyse use cases and requirements together; not in isolation.

Some selected users can help us understand the use cases when we interact with them. We need to ask the users questions and obtain their feedback on how they are intended to use a function that is expected to be in the IoT solution document.

In general, overall solution use cases need to be defined and elaborated with the input of all stakeholders of the solution, not just end-users. There may be different use cases for different stakeholders.

Use cases can also be determined based on the roles and personas involves in developing a solution. Personas represent fictitious characters, which are based on our knowledge of the users in the solution. Identifying personas and the use of them in our use case development and requirements analysis can be very beneficial. Agile methods have a strong focus on the use of personas. We also touch upon the personas in a later chapter on Agile methods.

To conclude, the importance of the use cases for IoT solutions, once the use cases are understood, precisely documented, and approved by all the relevant stakeholders, the requirements can be more explicit, decisions can be made more effectively, and the solution building blocks can be developed with more confidence.

Viability Assessment for IoT Solutions

Like any other IT project, performing Viability Assessments for IoT solutions is critical. Because of their complex and interrelated nature, the IoT ecosystems may pose multiple issues, risks and dependencies from various angles.

The purpose of conducting Viability Assessments is to focus on capturing, analysing and understanding the risks, issues, dependencies and assumptions associated with the solution.

Identified risks, issues, dependencies and assumptions need to be carefully analysed, sorted out and communicated to the stakeholders transparently.

After the analysis, the identified risks can be mitigated based on their likelihood and impact. We must first prioritise high impact and high probability risks and then move onto the medium and low likelihood and impact items.

In the Viability Assessment work-product, the issues must be clearly defined, and the options available to resolve the issues need to be pointed out. Further, these issues need to be assigned to relevant owners. Issues can include the current constraints and impediments which may adversely affect the successful completion of the IoT project at hand.

It is also necessary to define any dependencies, while there may also be some interdependencies between multiple components or building blocks of the solutions. The type of dependency and the potential impact needs to be articulated in the Viability Assessment work-product.

It is not only the IoT solution architects who develop Risks, Issues and Dependencies; the Project and Program Managers are also responsible for this task. Therefore, IoT Solution Architects must ensure that all technical and non-technical items are closely analysed, and their interdependencies adequately understood and documented. In addition, the Viability Assessment work-product developed by the IoT solution architects, as well as the one by the Project Managers, need to be integrated. If the issues, risks and dependencies are developed in isolation, things may fall into cracks, and no one can pick up those items, which can be harmful to the success of the project.

Architectural Models for IoT Solutions

Using several architectural models for IoT solutions can be instrumental. Some of the vital Architectural models which we can apply to the potential IoT solutions are Component Model, Operational Model, Performance Model, Security Model, Availability Model, Services Model and

Cost Model. These models need to be precisely documented, reviewed by the domain architects and governed by the Architecture Board or a Design Authority in the organisation.

Documentation of the architectural models can include both textual explanations and practical diagrams. For example, for a Component Model, all components and their relationships can be clearly illustrated in a diagram. The components and their functions can also be explained in detail. The diagrams can be useful communication tools for the models because the governance process for handling the solution architecture models requires presenting them to the Architecture Board or a Design Authority. With effective communication, obtaining technical assurance approvals can be faster and easier.

Approval for some of these models may also need to be obtained from the financial, commercial and other business stakeholders. For example, the Cost Model, Services Model and Availability Model can have content that requires financial approval. This means that, as solution architects, we not only deal with the technical aspect of an IoT solution but also the financial aspects.

Trade-Offs for IoT Solutions

Developing IoT solution architectures require making trade-offs to reach optimal solution outcomes. When making trade-offs, we need to consider several crucial factors, such as cost, quality, functionality, usability and many other non-functional items.

We can define a trade-off as creating a balance between two required yet incompatible items. In other words, a trade-off is a compromise between two options. It is possible to make a trade-off between quality and cost for particular items. For example, in an IoT solution, we may need to define the interfaces of an application, such as one way or bi-directional, and make required trade-offs for each option to reach the desired goal. To enhance usability, you may consider pre-built widgets for the IoT dashboards as a trade-off for cost.

We must make architectural trade-offs for dealing with uncertainties. For these types of trade-offs, techniques such as comparing, and contrasting can be beneficial.

Specifications for IoT Solutions

Like any other IT system, IoT systems are expected to deliver all their specifications correctly. Comprehensive configuration management for IoT solutions can be effective and useful when dealing with specifications.

In IoT solutions, a specification can be defined as the act of precisely identifying the ecosystem items. Since specifications require precision, delivering the right specification is an essential requirement for IoT applications and their associated critical business and emergency responses.

In IoT solutions, system specifications need to be accurate, reliable and fast when collecting data, communicating information, sharing data and making accurate decisions. Unreliable communication of the IoT specifications by various silos, inaccurate decisions made by those specifications, their cumbersome layout can lead to disastrous results when attempting to detail IoT solutions.

Finding the wrong specifications during the implementation and production support phase can be very cost-prohibitive due to massive re-work requirements. In addition to rework, the implications for SLAs can also cause a considerable amount of financial loss to the organisation.

Reference Architectures

A reference architecture is a re-usable solution or a design in a template format. The use of a reference architecture for IoT solutions can save us a considerable amount of time. Reference architectures are developed by experienced solution architects based on successful outcomes obtained from delivered solutions.

This means that we can trust the reference architectures as they were once successfully delivered. Following the same path as our customised specifications, these re-usable templates can save us a considerable amount of time and can improve the quality of our solutions.

As reference architectures are developed by experienced architects, they can also guide us in dealing with the unknown aspects of the solutions. Reference architectures can be used for various domains, can be combined to extend functionality and can be integrated for the final architecture solutions.

Some architects share their experiences for various reasons. For example, some architects share them for charitable give-back purposes or networking, or to boost their reputation and recognition in their industry. Whatever the reasons they share them, the reference architectures are invaluable resources for our planned solution architectures.

Open-source organisations produce many reference architectures in their domains. There are two primary sources for these reference architectures: either their members develop them as part of an open-source team, or some commercial companies donate their re-usable assets to the open-source organisations as reference architectures. The Open Group (TOG) is a typical example of this kind of open-source organisation.

Reference Architectures can be at a high-level or other detailed levels. A typical IoT reference Architecture at a high level can include essential points, such as Portal, Dashboard, API Management, Analytics, Services, Communications, Devices, Device Management, Security Management, Infrastructure and so on.

Reference Architectures are usually represented in diagrams with minimal text to explain the representations in the diagrams. Clarity is the main factor for a reference architecture. Reference Architectures usually are easy to understand and use.

In summary, while using reference architectures from other architects, to improve collaboration, it is also important to share our successful reference architectures with others, especially in the IoT area. The field is still evolving and many of our colleagues require Reference Architectures.

Chapter Summary and Take Away Points

Solution architects create or deal with multiple architectural work-products.

Solution architects need to understand the current environment, set the future environment and create a way to move from the current state to the future state.

Architectural thinking is an essential skill that architects from any domain must possess.

Requirements collection and analysis are fundamental architectural activities.

The requirements traceability matrix is a useful tool to track requirements across solution lifecycle.

The System Context is usually represented on a single page and is an ideal communication tool for the senior executives and business stakeholders to see the bigger picture of the solution.

Solution architects set the future environment by analysing and understanding the current environment.

The Component Model explains the components and their relationships in a solution.

The Operational model depicts how the solution can operate once it is in production.

Viability assessment includes essential architectural and technical issues, risks, dependencies and assumptions.

Architectural decisions must be approved by a governance body in the organisation.

IoT solutions touch upon almost all aspects of the architectural domain.

Functional aspects of a solution involve what the system offers to the consumers as functionality to be accomplished.

Non-functional aspects involve how the system can accomplish these functionalities, such as performance, availability, security, reliability, scalability, usability and so on.

IoMT (Internet of Mobile Things) is a sub-discipline of IoT.

IoT solution architects need to consider the scalability of devices, gateways, edge servers, cloud computer processes, storage capacity, analytics process and applications.

Interoperability means that heterogeneous devices and protocols need to be able to inter-work with each other.

Connectedness is a fundamental requirement of IoT.

A solution method can guide us toward which steps to take, in what order to take them and how to perform required tasks.

Our chosen method can help us reach our

destination most effectively.

The strategy of a solution hardly changes. Tactics can empower strategy.

Once the strategy is set, requirements analysis, validation and traceability need to be performed.

An architectural decision includes the possible options, selected option and the rationale for the selected option with clear recommendations.

The functional requirements can help formulate the use cases.

Use cases can also be determined based on roles and personas.

Risks, issues, dependencies and assumptions need to be carefully analysed.

Architectural trade-offs are required to be made for dealing with uncertainties.

For IoT specifications, unreliable

communication, slow speed and inaccurate decisions can lead to disastrous results.

A reference architecture is a re-usable solution or a design in a template format.

Reference architectures are developed based on successful outcomes.

Chapter 5: Security Considerations for IoT

Importance of IoT Security

When comparing all aspects of an IoT Solution, it is clear that security tops the list. In society, there is a great deal of fear surrounding the perception that IoT systems are easily hackable. To an extent, this fear is justifiable as the consequences of hacked IoT devices and services can often be life-threatening.

In relation to security, the other concern for IoT solutions is privacy. In IoT solutions, security and privacy go hand in hand. This means that while we are analysing and validating the security requirements, we also consider the privacy requirements.

Some IoT solutions could be compared to unchartered waters. As IoT solution architects, we need to understand the security pain points in these unchartered waters. The main reason for this prerequisite is that IoT is an emerging field; hence, there are still loopholes that should be systematically identified and addressed.

Therefore, we need to start asking powerful and open-ended questions to understand the security issues, risks, concerns, constraints and dependencies. At a high level, we may start posing the questions as to 'What are the security pain points in this solution?', 'What are the new technologies that may create risks?' and 'How can we address the identified risks?' among many more exploratory questions.

Of course, by asking many more questions, we prompt our minds to find effective resolutions for each concern. As IoT solution architects usually cover the breadth rather than depth in developing solutions, like any aspect of the solution, it is essential to have a security subject matter expert on hand to help delve into the details of security risks, issues, dependencies and constraints. These consulting subject matter experts can help validate our solution proposals. Therefore, it is highly recommended that the security subject matters experts review the security architecture of the solution and give their approval.

In addition to the security subject matter expert, the solutions are also reviewed by a security governance body in an organisation. The members of the governance body may review various aspects of security, such as identity management, authorisation, encryption, and many more.

Then, it is the IoT Solution Architect's role to ensure the recommended security actions fit into the overall solution. As you may have guessed, specialists of a specific domain are often unaware of the other domains and the overall solution. Understanding the importance of this point is critical as architects often make the assumption that subject matter experts in security know every aspect of the systems or solutions.

As IoT lead solution architects, we need to analyse and define the key security threats. Then, we need to propose solutions to address those threats in the Security Model of the IoT solution. These solution points in each solution building block need to be carefully reviewed by the security subject matter experts and peer-reviewed by other solution architects in the program or organisation who understand the security landscape for applications, middleware, data, hosting infrastructure, databases, network, storage and all other aspects of the solution. The following sections provide important considerations to create secure IoT solutions.

Analysing Security Requirements

IoT security and privacy requirements have specific characteristics due to unique communication mechanisms across borders reaching out multiple domains and extending to multiple ecosystems.

IoT Security and privacy requirements need to be analysed using reliable trust and assurance frameworks. These requirements need to consider the privacy laws in the geographies of the solutions that are developed. These requirements may not use traditional security controls. These requirements may have been developed in agility and may differ, state to state, country to country and continent to continent.

The analysed IoT security requirements for the IoT solutions need to be validated by the multiple stakeholders responsible for various aspects of the security in an organisation, project or entity. As mentioned before, the validation process also requires substantial input from security subject matter experts.

Once the IoT security requirements are validated, the security solution building blocks need to be traced to each validated requirement. Mandated requirements need to be given priority and proven to comply with the validated requests. Optional requirements should also be met as much as possible to strengthen the solution security aspects and features.

Security Risks, Issues, Dependencies and Constraints

Similar to other solution components,

conducting a security Viability Assessment is also essential to produce secure IoT solutions. A specific security Viability Assessment can help us analyse the critical security risks, issues, dependencies and assumptions methodically and systematically. This work-product can also help us find the optimal resolution points by prompting us on the fundamental aspects to address the viability items.

Although the lead IoT Solution Architect owns and initiates the security Viability Assessment work-product, the content details can be supported by multiple domain architects and security subject matter experts. For example, the security Viability Assessment work-product can consider the following essential security points:

- Security between the things (individual devices)
- Security from things to the Gateways
- Security from Gateways to the Edge devices
- Security from Edge devices or Gateways to Cloud, where the computing power is
- Security of data and databases integrated into the cloud
- Security between end-user devices and users

- Encryption requirements for data flow
- Security for application to middleware to IoT devices
- Mobile application to interfacing devices, such as mobile phones
- Digital Certificates
- Security of APIs Security of databases
- Cryptography
- Authentication
- Authorisation
- Identity of things
- Privacy of consumers
- Overall end to end infrastructure security

For each of these security points, it is necessary to undertake a deep-down critical review. The review points can be documented in the security Viability Assessment work-product under the titles of Risks, Issues, Dependencies and Assumptions. It is also useful to categorise IoT security risks as high, medium and low for impact and likelihood, while the severity of issues can also be categorised. Dependencies must also be clearly defined, and their impact needs to be articulated. Interdependencies amongst the security building blocks need to be identified and documented.

Following analysis, assumptions need to be validated and turned into risks, issues or dependencies. This means that the final version of the Viability Assessment must not have any assumptions as these issues need to be resolved before a solution is proposed. In other words, we cannot propose a solution when assumptions remain.

Creating a Comprehensive Security Model

Each IoT solution architecture must have a comprehensive Security Model. Considering a model as a proposed structure, typically on a smaller scale than the original, can be very useful to envisage the original security implementation through such an architectural model in the earlier phases. Models are useful tools to further elaborate the solutions for the next phases of the life cycle.

The solution document developed by the IoT solution architects needs to have a link to the comprehensive Security Model on the relevant chapters or sections.

The security model can cover an end-to-end walkthrough of the security aspects of the overall solution from all possible angles.

In the IoT Security Model, the problems need to be clearly defined. Then, recommended solutions with some alternatives, based on some useful scenarios, need to be provided. For example, it can include statements such as, 'If problem x occurs, then we recommend solution y because it has the benefits of xyz'. This problem can also be addressed by using the following xyz alternatives if the recommended solution is not viable for any reasons during the implementation period.

A well-documented security chapter, coupled with this level of preparedness, can add value to the quality of the solution and is very important in achieving the successful implementation and operational support of the solution.

Security Designs for Different Phases of the Solution

The security aspect of the IoT solutions needs to be considered for both the macro and micro design phases. In the macro-design phase, we developed several high-level designs. As mentioned earlier, the critical work-product to develop in this phase is a comprehensive Security Model. During the macro phase, it is difficult to identify the specific issues, risks and dependencies. Therefore, it is critical to have consulting security subject matter experts at the macro level.

However, during the micro design phase,

the subject matter experts need to include more details. For example, secure boot for a device can be part of the micro design. Security in IoT Protocols is another vital aspect to consider in the micro designs.

Layer by Layer Security Review Approach

Security threats exist at all layers, including physical, datalink, network, transport, session, t, and application layers. Each layer poses its own security challenges. Therefore, we need to check known security threats for each layer in a comprehensive way.

At the Data Link layer, some common IoT security threats can be MAC (Media Access Control) Flooding, Port Stealing, DHCP (Dynamic Host Configuration Protocol) attacks and ARP (Address Resolution Protocol) Flooding in the IoT ecosystem. Some known resolutions to the Data Link Layer attacks are the use of Intrusion Detection System, using Dynamic ARP Inspection and applying Root Guard.

Network layer security for IoT includes devices and appliances, such as routers, firewalls, and switches in the IoT ecosystem. Spoofing and DoS (Denial of Service) attacks are some of the most common network layer security threats. From a network security perspective, there are also several known threats for wireless devices. Some popular attacks for wireless devices can be Eavesdropping, Masquerading, Denial of Service and Message Modification.

At the Transport layer, the IoT security focus is on communication privacy and data integrity. The Transport Layer Security (TLS) is a protocol providing cryptography for end-to-end communications security over networks. This protocol is commonly used for Internet communications and online transactions. TLS is an IETF standard. TLS can prevent tampering, eavesdropping and message forgery. Another transport layer protocol to mention here is SSL (Secure Sockets Layer). SSL is another cryptographic protocol that is used to provide communications security over communication networks.

IoT Application layer security threats are pervasive. Some popular ones for our considerations are session hijackers, data exfiltration, zero-day vulnerabilities, CSRF (Cross-site request forgery), SQL Injections (SQLi), and XSS (Cross-Site Scripting) attacks. One of the popular solutions is the use of a WAF (Web Application Firewall. WAF is used to prevent attacks that take advantage of web application security flaws, such as cross-site scripting, SQL injections, and security misconfigurations.

A layer-by-layer security approach may also require engaging additional subject matter experts to help. For example, the network layer security threats can be better addressed by a network architect or a network specialist. In some organisations, the role of a network architect and specialist can be combined; hence, one person can take the role of the security subject matter expert.

Likewise, the application-level security concerns can be consulted to the application architects or specialists for that specific application if it is a complex application spanning multiple layers in the ecosystem.

Life Cycle Management

One of the observed key issues in IoT is limited guidance for the life cycle maintenance for the effective administration of IoT devices. When the IoT devices are not maintained well, and especially when security patches are not updated on a regular basis or when alerts happen, we can face ongoing security risks and issues.

To address this concern, architects need to develop a comprehensive Operational Model for the solution and include the life cycle maintenance principles and guidelines in the document. The preparation, review, and approval of the Operational Model can cause many issues to arise when the IoT solutions are implemented.

A proactive approach to maintaining a healthy IoT life cycle management can help address the risks, issues and dependencies at an earlier phase of the solution. This approach not only helps architects to address security issues related to life cycle management but also has a positive impact on the solution cost-effectiveness.

Privacy Concerns

Privacy is related to security. It is well-known that security risks can cause privacy issues. IoT privacy concerns can be complicated due to their nature; that is, they vary from country to country and are not always overt or obvious.

Therefore, to begin with, the IoT solution architects need to pay special attention to the privacy requirements. Then, using some of the above techniques, such as adding privacy concerns to the viability assessment and overall security documentation can be very useful.

Unique IoT Security Concerns

IoT technologies are rapidly changing,

expanding and transforming to different functions and shapes; hence, IoT technologies can have a tremendous impact on security. The previous security solutions may not meet newer solutions. We need fresh security approaches to address new risks, issues and dependencies.

The simplicity of Things for IoT Solutions is another essential point to be considered. Sophisticated IT security approaches may not suit the simple processor and tiny operating systems of these devices. Therefore, we need to develop new security approaches to address these unique situations.

For example, debug interfaces for IoT devices are well-known risks. Therefore, we must point out a piece of practical guiding advice in our solution security document — implementors should never leave any form of debugging access on a production device. Making these kinds of guiding principles as part of the solution policies can be very useful in the long run.

IoT Protocol Security

All layers of IoT protocols require the highest attention paid to security. Threats exist at all layers, including datalink, network, session and application layers. For example, lo6LoWPAN, by itself, does not offer any mechanisms for security. Hence, this requires special consideration.

Another example is MAC 802.15.4, which offers different security modes by utilising the Security Enabled Bit in the Frame Control field in the header. Security requirements include confidentiality, authentication, integrity, access control mechanisms and secured Time Synchronized Communications.

If a solution uses the RPL protocol, then there are some crucial points to consider. The RPL protocol has a specific level of security using a security field after the 4-byte ICMPv6 message header. Information in this field shows the level of security and the cryptography algorithm for the encrypted message. While making the viability assessments for the RPL protocol, we need to carefully consider well-known RPL attacks, such as Wormhole, Selective Forwarding, Hello Flooding, Sinkhole, Sybil, Blackhole and DOS (Denial of Service) attacks, which are the most popular.

Protocols for applications are also fundamental. We can provide an additional level of security to the application by using TLS or SSL as a transport layer protocol. Besides, end-to-end authentication and encryption algorithms can be used to handle different levels of security as required.

We also need to be aware of new protocol

security approaches being developed for resource-constrained IoT devices. Therefore, it can be instrumental in checking the progressing standards of the various IoT research and development projects.

Security by Blockchain-Enabled IoT

A recent addition to IoT security is the integration of blockchain to create highly secure and reliable connections. Blockchain enables the smart IoT devices to control, monitor and automate using the secure and reliable approach.

Blockchain is a distributed ledger that can record transactions amongst the parties involved in the process. It is an open-based security model. Blockchain prevents data to be manipulated in the life cycle. This is precisely what is needed in the IoT system security. Blockchain is, and will most likely be, the perfect fit for the IoT ecosystem.

Some research organisations, such as MIT, have worked with new frameworks such as ChainAchor, which is a blockchain-based IoT system. The proposed security framework includes layers of access that can keep out unauthorised devices or remove bad actors (such as a hacked device) from the network. It also includes cases for safely selling and removing devices from the blockchain.

Developing Criteria for Security Measures

With the help of Security subject matter experts in our project teams or organisations, we, as IoT solution architects, need to develop a set of criteria to take the required security measures in the solution documents.

The set of criteria needs to be objective and unique to the solution at hand. The security criteria can help us make a better assessment of the security risks, issues, dependencies and address the identified security concerns.

Besides, the security criteria serve to add extra rigour and diligence to the essential security measures. A set of criteria can also help the traceability of the security requirements in the solution building blocks.

Ethical Hacking for IoT Security

As IoT solutions are new and novel, there are several unknown aspects to these types of solutions. Therefore, another avenue for IoT security hardening is to introduce an ethical hacking approach to the operational model.

Ethical hacking is the act of locating vulnerabilities and weaknesses in IoT systems by reproducing the intentions and actions of ill-disposed hackers. Ethical hacking is also known as red teaming, intrusion testing and penetration testing.

During this design phase, as practical guidance and an additional measure, for example, after creating the operational model, some security experts with hacking capabilities can perform ethical hacking by conducting a fault-finding task on the security of the system.

Typically, ethical hacking is used in operational production systems; however, the early adoption of this method in the IoT lifecycle can be instrumental in addressing and identifying the unknown risks.

Security Hardening

Security hardening for IoT ecosystem can be an essential planning and administrative task. Hardening can be defined as the process of securing an IoT system by reducing its scope of vulnerability.

For example, we know that the bigger the scope of a system performing massive functions, the more complex and vulnerable the system can be. In general, a system with a single or fewer function can be more secure than a multipurpose one.

Some standard practices of hardening

include removing unnecessary services, removing unnecessary software functions, changing default passwords, creating strong passwords and removing unnecessary usernames or logins.

Cognitive Security for IoT

Introducing Cognitive Security to IoT solutions can be very beneficial. Cognitive security for IoT is the application of artificial intelligence technologies imitating human thought processes to detect security threats and protect the IoT ecosystems.

Cognitive IoT systems can efficiently learn from previous incidents in the ecosystem. They can also create scenarios using machine learning techniques. Some service providers, such as IBM, provide cognitive security via the IBM Watson solutions.

Systematic Security Walkthrough

A useful approach is to conduct a walkthrough of the IoT security components systematically starting with the user, the devices connecting to the gateways, the communication types from the gateways to the Cloud and the hosted applications in the Cloud.

Through this walkthrough, we can identify

essential security requirements and potential risks, such as the encryption requirements for Cloud traffic; security for message control; the security of remote access; the currency of devices, especially their firm-wares and user device gateway connection to the Cloud applications, etc.

Consumer Awareness

IoT consumers also need to be aware of the security risks. Even though these tasks seem to be geared towards that of the management level, this situation needs to be addressed at the architectural level. User security needs to be carefully defined and documented in the security solution document. Use cases related to user security need to be considered and mapped to the solution requirements.

Effective Authentication

Authentication requirements need to be carefully addressed. Authentication can be defined as the process or action of proving or showing something to be correct, genuine, or valid. In the IoT security context, the devices need to be authenticated by communications from various aspects of the system. IoT devices use various protocols and standards. Therefore, the chosen authentication methods must consider a variety of protocols and standards.

One of the vital authentication mechanisms of IoT is digital certifies. Digital certificates protect the data exchanged between the devices. Digital certificates are the foundation of a network's security, and thus protect its data, authenticate its devices, and create a trust for users interacting with the system.

End to End Encryption

Encryption is one of the most effective ways to achieve data security in the IoT ecosystem. Encrypted files cannot be read unless the secret key or passwords to decrypt them are known.

Encrypted data is also known as ciphertext. It is important to note that all communication between an IoT device and the Cloud environment needs to be encrypted.

To this end, using SSL/TLS protocols, where appropriate, can be very useful.

IoT High-Level Security Principles

As lead IoT solution architects, we can create our principles. For example, some of the crucial high-level security principles are to:

- Include security at all phases of the solution lifecycle,
- Apply for sensitive data review,
- Anonymise where possible and,
- Manage encryption keys securely.

The OWASP Foundation provides useful security principles for IoT solutions. OWASP stands for The Open Web Application Security Project. Some of the selected useful principles from this project are provided below and you can access the full list from the link provided in Appendix B.

- Assume a Hostile Edge
- Test for Scale
- Plan for the Worst
- Protect Uniformly
- Limit what you can
- Attackers Target Weakness

IoT Security and Compliance Framework

The IoT Security Foundation (IoTSF) is an organisation responsible for the security and compliance framework. This organisation provides IoT industry-based practices and offers educational conferences in the security and compliance domain of IoT. The organisation has a Compliance Framework that offers a compliance checklist. This checklist, when required at a high level, includes items such as:

- Business security processes
- Device hardware and physical security
- Device software and operating systems
- Device wired and wireless interfaces
- Authentication and authorisation
- Encryption and key management
- Web user interface
- Mobile applications
- Privacy
- Cloud and network elements
- Secure supply chain and production
- Configuration management

Chapter Summary and Key Points

IoT solution architects need to develop a comprehensive security document which covers the end-to-end security aspects of the overall solution from every possible angle.

IoT security covers both the macro and micro design phases.

Security threats exist at all layers of IoT

solutions.

IoT privacy issues vary from country to country and are not always obvious.

Never leave debugging access on a production device.

An additional level of security can be provided by using TLS or SSL as a transport layer protocol.

Blockchain enables smart IoT devices to control, monitor and automate through its secure and reliable approach.

Blockchain is a distributed ledger that can record transactions between the parties involved in the process.

The security criteria can help us make a better assessment of the security risks.

Introducing Ethical Hacking to IoT solutions can be beneficial.

Cognitive security is the application of artificial intelligence technologies that are designed to imitate human thought processes to detect threats and protect systems.

IoT consumers also need to be aware of the security risks.

One of the key authentication mechanisms of IoT is digital certificates.

All communication between an IoT device

and the Cloud needs to be encrypted.

The OWASP Foundation provides useful security principles for IoT solutions.

IoTSF is an organisation responsible for the security and compliance framework.

Chapter 6: Agile Approach for IoT Solutions

Purpose of Using Agile for IoT

Speed and quality are two key focus points in IoT solutions. The traditional view is that speed and quality are the competing aspects of product development. This means that the faster a product is developed, the less quality it may have. However, nowadays, speed is as important as quality. Consumers want products or services quickly; hence, the businesses are under tremendous pressure to serve their customers due to these ever-growing demands.

IoT solutions are usually created with utmost urgency due to their nature and the high expectations from the stakeholders. The product or service owners are under constant pressure to take their products and services to the market to stay competitive on the market. Consequently, this also puts much pressure on the IoT solution architects.

As mentioned earlier, it is a fact that consumers expect faster IoT devices. This trend is increasing, which thus puts the manufacturers and solution providers under pressure. We must keep in mind that the IoT devices require frequent updates for their software components, including firmware updates, also known as microcode, owing to increasing security concerns for IoT. As we can see from the security literature, the intelligence level of hackers is increasing.

Because of this agility trend in the industry and the focus to address the consumer demands, there is an ongoing need to deploy agile methods when finding IoT solutions. Agile approaches became the norm in IT environments, especially when creating IoT solutions and an IoT ecosystem in large organisations.

Agile also became popular in the manufacturing industry. There is a practice called "Agile Manufacturing with tools and processes of Agile approach designed for manufacturing. The aim of this practice is rapidly responding to customers, the market and innovations.

As IoT solution architects, we need to take part in this agile approach at the workplace. We are expected to provide quick architectural decisions and develop fast solution designs to meet the demands of the business.

This means that we have little time to analyse and make decisions at the macro level. This time constraint leaves no or minimal margin for mistakes. Therefore, IoT solution architects need to know the security, availability, performance and cost implications by heart.

In this case, to produce solutions in agility, substantial experience and in-depth knowledge matter for the IoT solution architects. Agility is one of the main reasons for this book to be created as an eye-opener for the IoT solution architects. The aim here is to prepare the IoT solution architects to meet these agility demands effectively.

How can we speed up developing IoT solutions? How can we produce hardware, software and combinations that are ready to market and serve the clients in agility? Moreover, how can we maintain operational quality while creating agility? The quick answer to these questions is to follow an established Agile solution method.

Using Agile methods is both the norm and the reality for IoT manufacturers, developers and service providers. The project management discipline adapted Agile very quickly; therefore, it is pervasive to see multiple agile projects in many organisations.

Not only the project managers but also the technical professionals are affected by agility trends in organisations. Therefore, IoT solution architects need to embrace Agile and know about Agile solution development techniques well and develop their solutions using adhering to the principles of this approach.

An Introduction to Agile Methods

In this section, I would like to provide a brief introduction to Agile methods at a high level. If you are new to Agile, you can learn some useful and standard Agile terms and concepts. This section, as a brief introduction, serves as a quick overview of Agile and the key concepts that solution architects use. Through this section, I aim to help those who don't have any exposure to Agile. You can safely skip this section if you have experience in using an Agile method.

As the IoT solution architects in the Agile projects, we can have multiple roles and responsibilities. For example, we can serve as a scrum master or as a scrum team member in an agile project.

We can also create different personas or a group of personas for our solutions. Personas represent fictitious people or characters, which are based on our knowledge of the users or consumers in the solution.

A scrum master can be a technical team lead role; however, it does have an element of project management to it. For example, a scrum master for a Sprint is expected to create and collect all User Stories, review them and publish them in an Agile board. In large organisations, a project manager usually undertakes this role; however, if an IoT solution is led by an Architect, then the lead Architect is expected to be the scrum master for that specific solution.

At a high level, some of the key concepts in an Agile project are being able to create Epics, write User Stories, put Stories to the Backlog, create solution artefacts and complete the Sprint successfully by producing an Acceptance Criteria. You have now five essential concepts of the agile: Epics, User Stories, Backlogs, Sprints and Acceptance Criteria. Let's briefly explain what they are and what they mean for solution architects.

Let's start with user stories. A User Story is a tool used in Agile solution development to capture a description of a solution feature from a user perspective. A User Story describes the type of user, what they want and why they want it. In other words, a User Story is a simplified explanation of the solution requirement. A collection of these User Stories establishes the requirements published in an Agile management tool.

The next important topic in Agile is Epic. An Epic can be a solution feature, customer request or a chunk of business requirements. The details of the features are defined in User Stories. An Epic can be defined as a group of work items that has a common objective. An Epic usually takes more than one Sprint to complete. In other words, Epics are big User Stories in nature.

The term spike is a kind of communication, such as a meeting or a phone call, to investigate how much time a User Story may take. This means that we may need to use a Spike for a User Story that cannot be estimated until the solution team performs a time-boxed investigation.

Another critical term for Agile is backlog. A backlog is a list of all tasks that need to be completed within a project. However, this list needs to be the desired features for the product or service component. It is a replacement for the traditional requirements specification artefact.

Backlog items can be described in technical terms or can be documented in the user stories format. A Backlog is used to prioritise features and understand which features to implement in priority order.

At the end of each sprint, there is also a Backlog Grooming (aka Backlog Refinement) activity. This activity is done to make sure the backlog is ready for the next sprint. By using this activity, Scrum team members can remove irrelevant user stories, create new stories or reassess the priority of existing stories, or even split user stories into smaller stories.

Sprint is a planned and time-boxed iteration of a continuous development cycle. Sprints usually take 2 weeks but could take up to a month. A timebox is a strictly defined time during which a task must be completed.

At strict Agile practices, once a period of two weeks or a month are consumed, the sprint is stopped because it is time-boxed. If the tasks and user stories cannot be completed at the determined time, the Sprint fails.

Agile practices pay much attention to the acceptance criteria. An Acceptance Criteria specifies a set of conditions that the solution must meet to satisfy the client. The product owner writes statements from the client's point of view that explain how a user story or epic must work.

For the User Story or the Epic to be accepted, it needs to pass the acceptance criteria; if not, it fails! The acceptance criteria must be written in clear, concise, and meaningful manner to bring the client and the solution team members on the same page.

Agile is a principle-oriented practice. Agile principles, in general, are common sense and can be a perfect match for IoT solutions. The most commonly used principles in Agile methods are:

- Embrace change

- Work as a team
- Transparency of work
- Have face to face time
- Measure progress
- Deliver frequently

Agile practices are methodical. There are several agile methods on the market. In this book, we only focus on the Agile Scrum Method and some Kanban terms as most pervasive methods. Some commonly used Agile methods in the industry are:

- Agile Scrum Method
- Kanban Method
- Crystal Method
- Lean Software Development Method
- Extreme Programming Method
- Dynamic Systems Development Method
- Feature Driven Development Method

There are proliferating numbers of Agile tools on the market. Interestingly, a new tool pops up almost every day! This is a good thing because each new Agile tool may introduce new functions, innovative approaches, and useful information management capabilities.

Agile teams responsible for IoT Solutions will most likely encounter tools that include the following: JIRA, Orangescrum, Progrgio, Binfire, Planbox, Nuvra, Teambook, ProofHub, Zoho Sprints, StoriesOnBoard, VivifyScrum, OneDesk, Agilelean, Wrike and Trello.

These are all useful tools for Agile methods. However, I found JIRA as one of the most effective tools in my technical projects. The JIRA dashboard has many useful functions and features. Some of its key features are issue types, workflows, screens, fields and issue attributes. For example, not all tools have these features. The dashboard on JIRA can be easily customised. We can also use JIRA to match our business processes.

It is also common to find some amazing terms in Agile teams, such as Chicken and Pig. A Chicken, in Agile terms, refers to someone who is involved in the project; however, he or she is not accountable for any specific deliverable. A Pig is considered someone who is committed and directly accountable for deliverables. This means that the solution architects are certainly categorised as Pigs (with no offence intended).

The term Kaizen is often repeated in Agile methods and means continuous improvement. Kaizen is the process of improving quality and efficiency by making small, incremental changes over time. Two key Kaizen activities for IoT solutions can be optimising workflows and reducing cycle times, which can result in increased productivity. Kaizen is a useful Agile term and principle to introduce to IoT ecosystems.

One inevitable aspect of Agile concerns the Daily Scrum, or Daily Stand-up sessions. These are brief communication and status check sessions managed by the Scrum Master. In Daily Scrum or the Daily Stand-up meetings, the team members share their progress, report constrains and make commitments for the current Sprint.

A Daily Scrum session includes focused conversation kept to a strict timeframe. Daily Scrum sessions are held at the same time on every business day, usually in the same location. The Scrum Task Board serves as the focal point of the Daily Scrum sessions. The Scrum Master asks three main questions to each team member: 1) What progress did you make today? 2) Do you have any roadblocks? 3) What is your plan for tomorrow?

The team members then provide quick and concise responses to these three questions. The scrum master keeps minutes of the Daily Scrums. The action points in these minutes are reviewed each day.

Considerations for Agile IoT Solutions

Agile methods have the principle of minimum functional delivery in a time-boxed manner. This means that the solutions make progress incrementally, and are designed, implemented and tested incrementally. The incremental progress makes the IoT solutions ideal candidates for the use of Agile methods.

Manufacturers or solution providers cannot just build and forget systems or solutions anymore, and moreover, Service providers are tightly dependent on manufacturers. This two-way integration requires a speedy delivery in terms of both manufacturing and service provision initiatives. Agile methods enable and facilitate this type of integration effectively.

Security is one of the critical themes of this book. From an Agile perspective, security is the primary factor behind the releases of ongoing updates for IoT devices that are used by the consumers. This security requirement caused the extension of software development lifecycle beyond deployment. Lifetime support has become the norm concerning the emergence of connected devices which pose dependencies on themselves.

Agile methods help the IoT developers to have a reasonably manageable development schedule for the IoT solutions. From hindsight, we know that the waterfall method takes longer and cannot serve the demanding requirements of the IoT lifecycle and ecosystem. More importantly, IoT Architects hardly ever use the waterfall methods because by using the waterfall methods, which are cumbersome and time-consuming, they cannot meet the demands of the architectural solution life cycle.

Agile methods not only focus on incremental development and shorter lead times but also strongly focus on automating everything possible in the shortest possible time, thereby reducing human intervention and errors, and hence, increasing quality. For example, automating software updates can simplify the overall currency process from multiple ends, such as developers, service providers and the consumer points of views.

Agile methods also focus on simulators for automation of tests which are not possible in the production systems or the consumers' home. This type of automation used by Agile methods, which is a simulation, helps speed up test times as close to real-life situations as possible. Process Automation (PA) is a commonly used Agile practice in manufacturing environments.

Another benefit of Agile for IoT Architecture is that Agile methods embrace collaboration amongst multiple teams by breaking silos. The required communication flows faster and in an integrated way; or in other words, more coherently. The collaboration approach in Agile is also ideal for the requirements of IoT for the extended lifecycle of projects with multiple stakeholders.

The ability to simulate tests is critical to the performance of agile for the IoT solutions because it is difficult to test a connected device within the context of the full system. However, with the power of simulations, organisations can automate functionalities within the simulator and then thoroughly test them. In doing so, they can parallelise, scale and reconfigure as needed and then send the test failures to developers so they can solve the issues at hand. As Agile methods focus on providing more rapid development and a feedback loop, developers can quickly fix bugs and contribute new codes that have been tested and validated. Therefore, IoT Architects mandate Agile methods in their governance models, governance work-products or solution documents.

The use of sprints in Agile is a crucial point for IoT solution development and ecosystem enhancement activities. The sprint approach breaks down an IoT deployment into smaller and more easily manageable initiatives, which can take place in the shortest possible lead time. Sprint is unlike the solution phases in waterfall methods, which have long time frames and open-ended deployment schedules. Agile Sprints make it easier to understand the requirements, deliverables and deployment efforts from the standpoint of all stakeholders.

The use of Agile methods for solution architectures has a positive impact on solution quality, time and budget. Furthermore, it has a positive impact on the performance, availability and economic aspects of IoT. Performance and availability improvements boost the quality of solutions and reduce the cost of solutions.

Chapter Summary and Key Points

Using Agile methods has become famous for IoT manufacturers, developers and service providers.

Agile is an essential and collective approach to IoT solutions.

A User Story is a simplified explanation of the requirement.

An Epic can be defined as a group of work items that has a common objective.

A Backlog is used to prioritise features and understand which features to implement according to priority.

Sprint is a planned and time-boxed iteration of a continuous development cycle.

Acceptance Criteria specifies conditions that the solution must meet to satisfy the client.

Kaizen means continuous improvement.

Daily Stand-up sessions are brief status check session managed by the Scrum Master.

Agile methods help the IoT developers to have a reasonably manageable development schedule for IoT solutions.

Agile methods focus on incremental development and automating everything possible in the shortest possible time.

Agile methods embrace collaboration amongst multiple teams by breaking silos.

Chapter 7: Availability & Performance for IoT Solutions

Availability & Performance Overview

Solution availability can be defined as the probability a solution is functioning when needed and under normal operating conditions. The critical factors for availability are well functioning of all system components, such as infrastructure, applications and communications. The bottom line for availability is that the weakest points in a system component or group of components need to be well-thought-out.

Solution availability is closely related to solution performance. Solution performance can be defined as the amount of planned work accomplished by a solution in a defined timeframe. The critical indicators for excellent performance are accuracy, efficiency and speed of executions.

IoT solution architects focus on both the availability and performance of the products or services created by these types of solutions in an integrated manner. The availability and performance of products and services are the day-to-day demands made by the consumers of IoT solutions and services.

In architectural vernacular, both availability and performance are non-functional aspects of the solutions. In fact, availability and performance are the key non-functional requirements which need to be validated, approved and traced in the requirements analysis phase. Therefore, we know that availability and performance models and designs are key architectural activities in the architectural life cycle of the solutions. We must pay supreme attention to these two non-functional aspects of the IoT solutions.

Both availability and performance are part of the solution technical quality assurance process. Each system or solution building block need to have proper availability and performance tests based on selected criteria by the business users, solution owners or other key stakeholders. IoT solution architects provide significant input to the availability and performance tests once the solution is about to be implemented.

It is a fact that IoT solutions require high availability and high performance. Therefore, IoT solution architects need to spend a considerable amount of time in ensuring IoT availability and performance solutions.

Adequate time must be captured in the solution cost model and this allocated time should not be compromised due to widespread cost-cutting exercises in some projects and programs. As IoT solutions architects, we must be adamant on this point and articulate the importance of performance and availability investments to the sponsoring executives.

Availability of IoT solutions includes software and hardware levels being provided at any time (on-demand) and anywhere for service subscribers in a utility-based model.

Software availability means that the service is provided to anyone who is authorised to use it in their devices. Hardware availability means that the existing devices are easy to access and are compatible with IoT functionality and protocols. Besides, these protocols should be compact to be able to be embedded within the IoT constrained devices.

In the following sections, we briefly touch on the critical factors for availability and performance in creating, developing, implementing and testing IoT solutions.

Importance of an Availability & Performance Model

To design a high-performance and highly available IoT solution, the IoT solution architects need to produce diligent performance and availability models, which then require a peer review. In addition, these models need to be reviewed for technical accuracy and details by the subject matter experts in the team or organisation. These models need to be approved by a governance body.

Once the availability and performance models are approved by a governance body, such as the Architecture Board or a Design Authority, and when the solution is in the detailing phase, the lead IoT solution architects need to apply established design principles. Applying solution availability and performance principles can enable to address the detailed requirements for both availability and performance models.

Availability and Performance models can be in various formats, such as visual, textual or combinations of both. They can be explained in detail and illustrated with diagrams. They can also include performance walk-throughs and what-if scenarios.

Top-down & Bottom-up Approach

A top-down approach to IoT availability and performance is essential. This approach may start with a strategy and later include high-level design, detailed designs, implementation plans and tests. This means that availability and performance are considered at all levels of the

IoT solution life cycle.

Besides, availability and performance development also requires a bottom-up approach. For example, IoT solution architects who are hands-on start with the end-product and walk back through the design and architecture phases. This bottom-up is also an instrumental approach for enabling reliable performance and high availability solutions.

We can also use a reverse engineering approach to performance and availability. Reverse engineering can be applied as a bottom-up approach to both availability and performance, starting with small units making the more significant components.

Performance & Availability Integration

Performance and availability go hand-in-hand. They are interrelated and integrated for the quality of IoT solutions. The availability model can have related item for performance model and the performance model includes availability-related items.

For example, poor performance in a production service can adversely impact availability. Low availability adversely affects the desired performance. Therefore, both performance and availability requirements need to be analysed and solved using an integrated approach.

While developing service level agreements for an IoT solution, both availability and performance models must be considered in an integrated way.

Service & System Management for Performance & Availability

It is a fact that a massive number of IoT devices require proper hosting in well-managed and governed data centres supported with high-availability principles in a 24-by-7 approach. This includes disaster recovery and service management plans.

Hosting IoT solutions (products and services) in established data centres need to be part of the IoT solution architecture. In the service management component of the solution, we can guide on hosting environments.

The availability and performance requirements of IoT solutions can also be improved by designing well-functioning systems and service management architecture. For example, monitoring, alerting and event management solutions can be part of this system and service management architecture.

The monitoring of operational performance and availability can also be solved and mandated in the IoT solution architecture documents. Including the process and tools for monitoring performance and availability in the service management solution document can be useful.

IoT solution architects also need to be aware of a range of IoT tools that can be easily plugged in to manage the services and systems. These tools can be implemented based on IoT use cases obtained from various stakeholders and consumer types.

Constraints & Impediments

Dealing with constraints and impediments may have a critical impact on performance, availability and cost. As IoT solution architects, we need to focus on identifying impediments and constraints in the ecosystem.

The constraints and impediments can take place in various layers of the protocols, in actual devices and other components of the ecosystem. An example of a constraint for IoT solutions can be commonly experienced in networks. IoT devices are connected to multiple networks.

The network communications may go through firewalls and other security mechanisms, such as network address translations or proxy appliances. In this specific case, a firewall may block necessary traffic unintendedly. This kind of impediment may have serious implications for availability, performance and cost associated with meeting service level agreements.

Both in Availability and Performance Model work-products, it will be useful to have a section about constraints and impediments. In this section, constraints and impediments need to be articulated comprehensively, and the resolutions need to be clearly defined, reviewed and agreed, and the proposed actions approved.

IoT Sensors and EndPoints

IoT ecosystems are complex. This complexity has a significant impact on performance and availability. We know that the complexity for performance occurs in the IoT ecosystem because the IoT devices are multiple points that are linked, such as to end-point devices, to mobile applications and the cloud platforms.

Managing all these devices and keeping track of the failures, configurations and performance of such a large number of devices can be a challenge in IoT solutions. Providers need to manage the fault, configuration, accounting, availability, performance and security of their interconnected devices. These providers need to account for every aspect of these devices.

There is a continuous integration need for multiple components and delivery obligations for the demanding consumers of the IoT solutions in the ecosystem. End-points can be in geographically-distant places.

The communication between end-points and other components of the IoT systems requires careful availability and performance analysis. For example, the distance at network-level communications can cause latency. Let's elaborate on latency as it is a critical point for performance and availability.

Network Bottlenecks

Network bottlenecks adversely affect availability, performance and the cost of products or services in productions, making the service level agreements challenging to meet. Network bottlenecks can be very harmful. Apart from latency related to the distance that we mentioned in previous sections, several other factors are causing the network bottlenecks.

Some common causes of network bottlenecks are malfunctioning devices, having an excessive number of devices connected to the networks, limited bandwidth and overcapacity for server utilisation.

In IoT solutions, we need to engage an

end-to-end network architect or several network specialists who specialise in various aspects of the network where there may be bottlenecks. The best practice is to consider these well-known bottlenecks and provide a high-quality capacity plan for the network by obtaining proactive input from the network subject matter experts.

IoT Gateways

Gateways can act as intermediaries between Edge Devices and the Cloud. Gateways can offer additional location management services. Performance and availability also require the consideration of endpoints and gateways. Endpoints consist of physical sensors. These sensors send messages to the IoT platform via gateways, which are fundamental components to the ecosystem.

The main reason these gateways are so important is that the objects can take place in multiple locations due to their nature — for example, a moving object, such as a transport vehicle with built-in IoT sensors. The messages created by these moving objects are stored by the gateways and delivered by the gateway to the IoT platforms in the ecosystem. The moving devices can connect and reconnect to the gateways using various data link protocols.

The moving objects require the gateways

to be dynamic servers with changing conditions and new communication requirements.

Impact of Massive IoT Data

IoT devices generate massive amounts of data on an ongoing basis. These data sets go to the full data management life cycle; for example, in storing, analysing, re-building, and archiving. The amount of data produced by IoT devices require careful performance, scalability and availability measures.

We need to simulate the actual workload models based on the functional and non-functional requirements. We also need to consider historical data and future growth as part of the requirements analysis for performance.

Data collection via IoT sensors needs to be planned carefully. First, we need to determine the type of physical signals to measure. Then, we need to identify the number of sensors to be used and the speed of signals for these sensors in our data acquisition plan.

In addition to the challenges of massive data, application usage patterns are also an essential factor for performance. In particular, the processors and memory of the servers hosting the IoT applications need to be considered carefully using benchmarks.

Using benchmarks for application, data and infrastructure, we need to create an exclusive IoT performance model and a set of test strategies. The IoT performance model mandates more data storage capacity, faster processes, more memory, faster network infrastructure and so on. While in the traditional performance models we mainly consider user simulations, in the IoT Performance models, we also consider the simulation of devices, sensors and actuators.

From a data management perspective, it is paramount to be aware of data frequency shared amongst devices. This means that not only the amount of data produced and processed but also accessed and shared frequently by multiple entities of the IoT ecosystem.

The monitoring of these devices also creates a tremendous amount of data. If we always add the alerts and other system management functions to keep these devices well-performing and available, we need to have a comprehensive performance model, including the system and service management of the complex IoT ecosystem.

Protocols and Communications

From the perspectives of protocol and communication, the performance simulations require the analysis of new protocols in this ecosystem. These IoT protocols are relatively new and not yet fully established to meet the requirements of traditional performance testing tools. The IoT protocols can be varied, such as short-range or long-range. They can also be low or high bandwidth. We know that these IoT protocols are evolving; therefore, their specifications may change frequently.

The ongoing changes in protocols introduce another challenge to the supportability of the protocols. This emerging condition for protocols needs to be considered in performance testing, performance monitoring and availability solutions. We discuss these protocols in the section about the component model and the IoT ecosystem section in this book.

More about network protocols impact on performance are provided in previous sections. Just a quick recap, as IoT devices spread across the globe, network access and latency need to be included as part of the Performance and Availability Models. Specific testing needs to be performed to simulate latency across multiple devices hosted in a different part of the globe in the ecosystem.

Application Performance and Availability

To discuss the importance of application architecture in IoT, it is essential to note that the requests and responses flow from multiple directions and the addition of multiple devices to the ecosystem. Responses from multiple devices create their requests and responses to the application, as well as those to the user and other system responses. These mixed device, application and user responses create large amounts of traffic, which, consequently, affect the performance measures.

This complexity can be managed through decent architectural planning and the development of the performance model. We need to bear in mind that the typical business applications in the back-office and the IoT intelligence applications in the Cloud can be factored into the performance model development.

IoT Development Tools

IoT solution architects need to understand the IoT development tools available to them and select the most relevant tool or toolset for their solutions.

Some tools may provide additional considerations for performance and availability. These tools need to be evaluated based on the requirements analysis.

Some standard commercial and open source IoT development tools on the market are Eclipse IoT, Node-RED, Device Hive, Tessel2, Arduino, OpenSCADA, PlatformIO, Raspbian, IBM Watson, and Kinomo Create.

Chapter Summary and Key Points

Performance can be defined as the amount of planned work accomplished by a solution in a defined timeframe.

Availability can be defined as the probability of a solution functioning when required and under normal operating conditions.

Performance and availability models can be visual, textual or combinations of both.

A top-down approach to IoT availability and performance is essential.

An IoT solution also may require a bottom-up approach.

Performance and availability go hand-in-hand for the quality of IoT solutions.

IoT devices require proper hosting in well-managed and governed data centres.

Monitoring, alerting, and event management solutions need to be part of the system and service management architecture.

Constraints also need to be carefully considered for availability and performance.

The amount of data produced by IoT devices require careful performance, scalability and availability measures.

We can simulate actual workload models based on functional and non-functional requirements.

The IoT performance model mandates more data storage capacity, faster processes, more memory and faster network infrastructure.

Not only is the amount of data produced and processed important but also accessed and shared frequently by multiple entities of the IoT ecosystem.

IoT protocols are evolving; hence, their specifications may change frequently.

Chapter 8: Effective Cost Model for IoT

Importance of Cost Awareness for IoT solution architects

Cost is an essential consideration for producing and maintaining IoT products, solutions and services. Every aspect of IoT solutions requires cost considerations. As IoT architects, we need to be cost-aware and focused on our day-to-day tasks at any phase of the solution lifecycle.

We, as IoT solution architects, can save or waste money based on our choices and decisions. This means that our decisions play an essential role in the cost-effectiveness of an IoT solution.

Solution Architectures may play different roles in various phases of the IoT solutions lifecycle. High-quality solution architectures can have a positive impact on cost, such as cost-saving in the long run. Bad quality of architecture can have a negative impact on costs, such as cost of rework, redesign, faults, poor performance, low availability, and punitive SLAs.

IoT solutions require careful consideration

of Service Level Agreements (SLAs) and associated service-level costs. The next session explains the costs related to SLAs.

Service Level Costs

There are extensive infrastructure and maintenance costs associated with large data centres, server farms and centralised clouds. These centralised infrastructure components can make the solutions more viable from a cost perspective; however, a single failure or defect in a device a group of devices serving the consumer can affect the service levels and could lead to high costs for the service providers.

Service levels are usually based on the Availability and Performance of the systems. Low availability and poor performance are detected by the SLAs and organisations breaching the agreements pay the agreed penalties.

Service downtime costs can be very high and cause excessive penalties for service-level breaches by organisations. Service Level breaches also have a strategic adverse effect on an organisation's product and services. For example, downtimes in services or defects in products can result in poor client satisfaction.

IoT solution architects need to pay attention to the SLAs from the early stages of the solution life cycle. The higher the quality of the solutions, the easier it is for SLAs to meet when the solutions are in production and the operational state.

Some of the key considerations could be autonomous condition monitoring and remote maintenance. There are specialist solutions regarding these trending techniques; hence it can be useful to engage automation specialists for the design of these unique features in our solutions.

Service level management is also crucial in IoT organisations as one of the biggest fears of IoT business executives is if IoT performance problems damage their organisations' revenues.

Cost Implications for Availability & Performance

Availability and performance topics that are close to the hearts of the solution architects have a significant impact on the costs, which are close to the hearts of business executives. This means that architectural diligence and decisions for availability, performance and security can positively impact cost in the long run.

If architecture is not robust, and if not enough thought is put into architecture at the earlier phases, then, most likely, the cost of the projects can increase; besides, the situation can worsen when solutions are deployed, and the support systems go live.

Poorly performing products and services not only increase the cost of supportability but also may harm an organisation's reputation. For example, unsatisfied clients can cause business loss.

Solution Costs

Architects need to find ways to make IoT inexpensive, affordable and lowering the cost gradually without compromising quality. Quality considerations are the key themes of this book such as availability, performance, security and agility.

Some may argue that making solutions cost-effective without compromising quality is not possible as a considerable number of trade-offs are made in the architecture development phase.

However, the solution cost can be reduced by making a trade-off with a methodical approach by obtaining collaborative input from business and technology departments and using the Agile approach appropriately. The quality of the solution can be increased to provide highly available and high-performance solutions.

One key consideration is to create the Bill

of Materials (BOM) once the solution strategy is set and all high-level design artefacts are complete. Beware that there may be tremendous pressure from project managers and procurement staff to generate an upfront BOM; however we can point out that without architecture is approved no BOM can be released. This simple input from the solution architect can save a considerable amount of funds to the IoT project or save wasting tight budgets.

Cost for Devices

Devices have several cost items associated with their production and support. Among them, one of the critical considerations for the cost of devices is related to their use of energy power; for example, battery life, battery size and the way the device uses the energy for sustainability.

Also, it is worth noting that the cost of changing the battery for thousands of devices can be very high, and the process to change them can be very time-consuming.

IoT solution architects may need to make a design choice concerning battery life. Ideally, the battery life should last a few years rather than a matter of months or weeks. In fact, as a rule of thumb, it is believed that anything under 10 years is not considered sustainable and cost-effective.

Another design choice can be the use of energy harvested or battery-provided power. For example, if solar energy is used to charge batteries, it may have a long-term, positive impact on cost.

Cost Impact of IoT Protocols

The IoT protocols present a considerable amount of cost implications on the solutions. To this end, we need to consider cost-effective protocols with the effective use of energy. One architectural decision could be the use of low power, wide-area network communication protocols.

Another consideration is the use of cellular connectivity protocols. Interestingly, cellular IoT connectivity protocols are more comfortable to set up and provide better reliability. From the security point of view, the protocols also allow the device owners to be in control of the data.

The use of wireless mesh network topology using mixed protocols can also be very cost-effective and can aid in producing high-performing and high availability solutions. The mixed protocols in this topology connect and extend the radio signals for routing covering more prominent zones. They create a reliable network.

The more reliable the network, the better performance they pose. For example, the use of Zigbee can be a cost-effective, contributing factor to the solution because Zigbee delivers low-latency communication, and it is a low-cost and low-power wireless mesh network standard. Zigbee is used for battery-powered devices in wireless control applications.

Contribution to Cost-Effectiveness

Solution architects contribute much to the cost-effectiveness of the solutions in the form of both products or services.

IoT solution architects can make strategic decisions for the quality of products and services at the initial phases. We know that effective architectures can have a positive impact on solution productivity.

To conclude, effective and timely architectural decisions, producing quality work-products (especially Availability, Performance and Security Models), careful analysis of requirements, well-understood use cases and other architectural practices on the solution can contribute to the cost of solution considerably.

Chapter Summary and Key Points

Every aspect of IoT solutions requires cost

considerations.

High-quality solution architectures can have a positive impact on cost.

Service downtime costs can be very high and cause excessive penalties.

Downtimes in services or defects in products can result in poor client satisfaction.

IoT performance problems can damage revenues.

Through appropriate use of the Agile approach, the cost can be reduced by making trade-offs with a methodical approach and collaborative input from business and technology departments.

The cost of changing the battery for thousands of devices can be very costly and time-consuming.

Cellular IoT connectivity protocols are easier to set up, and they provide better reliability.

Zigbee delivers low-latency communication and it is a low-cost and low-power wireless mesh network standard.

Chapter 9: Further Learning for IoT Solution Architects

Like for any other professionals, learning never ends for the IoT solution architects. Continuous learning is of utmost importance for IoT solution architects. Solution architects usually cover breadth rather than depth, as opposed to the specialists. This means that they need to understand every aspect of the solution at a high level.

However, there are times when the IoT solution architects are required to know specialist information; however, most of the time, solution architects work with subject matter experts (SMEs) to validate their solution components or solution building blocks in details.

However, some architects working with IoT systems may also want to cover greater depth and produce more outstanding results in their architectural engagements. For those who want to cover depth in IoT, we recommend learning additional topics in the IoT domain by diving into special domains such as Machine Learning, Data Science, API Design and Middleware Design.

There are many emerging interdisciplinary

Bachelor and Master of Science and Engineering degrees that focus on the Internet of Things. These academic IoT courses cover mobile device applications, wearables and ubiquitous sensors, all of which are rapidly emerging with the deployment of new networks and specialised hardware.

In addition to academic degrees, there are also short courses offered by various Universities and Training organisations. For example, MIT offers a course titled Internet of Things: Business Implications and Opportunities. There are also several certification courses available, such as Internet of Things (IoT) Certification by Curtin University. For example, the University of Technology Sydney (UTS) offers a course on IoT Future Masterclass, and the University of Oxford offers Data Science for the Internet of Things certification.

There are also certifications and education programs available for IoT professionals. Undertaking these courses and certifying the skills can most likely help the architectural work in developing, designing and architecting IoT solutions.

From the IoT industry perspective regarding relevant skill sets, there are several emerging IoT-related digital badges offered by various companies, such as IBM, Microsoft, PwC, and so on, as can be viewed from the Acclaim web site.

An organisation called Arcitura Education is a leading global provider of progressive, vendor-neutral training and certification programs. This organisation offers a certification program called 'A Certified IoT Architect'. Arcitura Education's website contains the following statement: 'A certified IoT architect has demonstrated proficiency in IoT technology architecture, protocols, mechanisms and security, and has acquired specialised skills to assess, design and deliver real-world IoT solutions'. More information can be obtained from Arcitura web site.

Microsoft is another organisation providing certification in IoT. For example, *Microsoft Professional Program Certificate in Internet of Things (IoT)* covers high-level topics such as IoT Device Configuration and Communication, IoT Data Analytics and Storage, Business Intelligence for IoT Solutions, Predictive Analytics for IoT Solutions and IoT Architecture Design and Business Planning.

The course on Certified Internet of Things Professional (CIoTP) by GSTF focuses on the core technologies behind the Internet of Things. The organisation claims that 'This certification leverages and explores the middleware for IoT, Machine learning for Intelligent IoT, Data Science for Intelligent IoT, Analytic engine for IoT, Big data platform for IoT, API design considerations for IoT, IoT standards and Management of IoT, which makes a world fully connected'.

Working with Popular IoT Vendor Technologies and Environments

As the vendor-agnostic author of this book, my aim is not to recommend, endorse or criticise any specific vendor environments or technologies, but rather, to create awareness by introducing them and emphasising their importance in developing architectural solutions. In my view, IoT solution architects not only need to understand vendor solutions; however, they also need to be vendor-agnostic to develop architectural solutions even though they work for a specific vendor.

Each vendor environment is unique, each with its own proprietary, open-source and combined technologies and tools. It is the architect's responsibility to understand the specific environment that they are working on and the specific technologies that they are using in their solutions. Interestingly, many vendors also partner with other vendors to create synergetic solutions and services.

IoT solution architects need to understand the environments in which they develop solutions. For example, if an IoT solution is based on Microsoft technologies, the IoT Solution Architect needs to know about Microsoft Azure data platform services, such as SQL, Data Warehouse, Databricks, Data Lake, Azure Data Factory, HDIinsights, Stream Analytics, IoT Hub, and Azure Machine Learning.

Another large organisation providing IoT services and platforms are AWS (Amazon Web Services). AWS IoT provides device software, control services and data services. Amazon FreeRTOS is an operating system for microcontrollers that makes small, low-power edge devices easy to program, deploy, secure, connect and manage.

There are also other services by AWS, such as AWS IoT Greengrass—a software running local compute, messaging, data caching, sync, and machine learning inference capabilities on connected devices in a secure way. More information about AWS IoT Services can be obtained from Amazon IoT site.

Chapter Summary and Key Points

Learning for IoT is a continuous process.

Certification can be useful to improve skills and prove experience.

There are many academic and industry courses to learn about the theoretical and practical aspects of IoT.

IoT solution architects cover breadth rather

than depth.

Understanding Data Science principles, learning about API Design, Middleware Design, and Machine Learning can be useful for IoT solution architects.

IoT solution architects need to be vendor-agnostic when developing solutions.

IoT solution architects also need to understand the commercial environments in which they develop solutions.

Chapter 10: Conclusions and Actions for IoT Solution Architects

Summary and Conclusions

In the following sections, I provide a summary of the key points discussed in the earlier chapters of this book. This summary can reinforce your learning by focussing on the key points in previous chapters.

Consumers are in urgent need of IoT solutions. These solutions are expected to be up and running all the time without any glitches. They are also wanted to be cheap and affordable. This simple consumer behaviour dictates the IoT solutions and the duties of IoT solution architects. This typical consumer behaviour translates to the architectural practices as highly available, well-performing, agile and economical solutions.

The IoT solutions that we produce have a significant impact on our society. They are used at home, in the workplace and any other place where human interactions take place. These IoT solutions change the things we perceive and experience and add new meaning to our lives.

IoT is considered a paradigm shift in information technology. The IoT solutions that we produce as products or services can have human-like senses. They can imitate hearing, seeing, thinking and even decision making. We create these solutions to make people's lives easier. However, ironically, they may also clutter our lives and create additional complexity and even safety, security and privacy risks.

The technology components that make IoT a reality are sensors, actuators, electronics, other hardware like servers, storage units, network, communication software, middleware and applications. Adding the power of the internet to traditional IT in a unique way is what creates the IoT. This unique approach, under the umbrella name IoT, has attracted a large amount of consumer and business attention and is growing exponentially.

The value proposition of IoT in terms of collecting vast amounts of data from various means and devices, and then building services upon analyses of these valuable data, creates an enormous potential for business and economy.

Our IoT solutions can also have an impact on creating better insights for consumers. This impact can stem from the cognitive analysis of combined structured, unstructured, dynamic and static data sets from a myriad of devices. These datasets can be used for several applications, such as home entertainment, home automation, industrial control, remote control, medical data collection, wearables, smart city, smart grid, industrial internet, connected cars, connected health, smart retail, smart supply chain and smart farming, among many others.

Considering the ecosystem as a complex network and interconnected system, the IoT ecosystems are usually made of simple or complex multiple systems, components, sub-components, integrated, single-tasking or multitasking elements. The standard components of the ecosystem are the Things, Sensor Devices, The Edge (Edge and Fog Computing), Gateways, the Internet, Communications, Protocols, the Cloud, Analytics, Applications and Consumers.

Architecting the IoT solutions methodically and harmoniously in the ecosystem can produce positive outcomes for products or services. There are special considerations for IoT solutions, such as the careful use of Gateways. IoT gateways can minimise the high volume of data generated by the sensors. The data from the sensors are captured in analogue format and can be heat, light, motion, voltage, vibration, and so on. These kinds of analogue data must be converted into a digital format for further processing. Data Acquisition Systems (DAS) perform data aggregation and conversion functions.

IoT gateways are communication points between sensors and the Cloud. Data coming from the sensors pass through the Gateways to reach to the Cloud. IoT gateways can provide additional security mechanisms, such as encrypted transmissions.

In this methodical architecture, we also need to carefully consider Edge Devices and the Cloud. Processing data can be performed by the edge devices for efficiency. Use of the IoT Cloud facilitates the data integration of the systems. IoT Cloud can improve the security, availability and performance of the IoT systems. Edge computing can do the filtering for the Cloud to focus on the real data.

Application of integration and the use of patterns in IoT ecosystems are essential, enabling factors. We can use APIs to integrate devices, applications, data and the cloud systems easily and effectively. Common IoT communication patterns are Information Flows, Queries, Commands and Notifications.

Use of standards is also an essential factor affecting IoT ecosystems. IoT solutions require several standard protocols and newly developed IoT specific protocols. There are several standards developed by various organisations, such as IEEE, IETF and ITU.

IoT solution architects think strategically and create multiple architectural work-products. The strategy of a solution does hardly change. Tactics empower strategy. IoT solution architects need to understand the current environment, set the future environment and create a way to move from the current state to the future state. Architectural thinking is an essential skill that architects in any domain must possess. An architectural decision includes the possible options, selected option and the rationale for the selected option with clear recommendations.

Once the strategy is set, requirements analysis, validation and traceability need to be performed. Requirements analysis is a fundamental architectural activity. The requirements traceability matrix is a useful tool to track requirements. The functional requirements can help formulate the use cases. Use cases can also be determined based on roles and personas.

Once requirements are understood and approved, the IoT solution architects create the System Context, which is usually represented on a single page and is an ideal communication tool for the senior executives and business stakeholders to see the big picture of the solution. The Context and other high-level communication diagrams can be extracted from Reference Architectures. A reference architecture is a re-usable solution or a design in a template format. Reference architectures are developed based on successful outcomes.

IoT Solutions require the development of several models. The component model explains the components and their relationships in a solution, while the operational model illustrates how the solution can operate when it is deployed. A viability assessment includes the critical architectural and technical issues, risks, dependencies and assumptions. Architectural decisions must be understood by all stakeholders and approved by a governance body in the organisation.

IoT solutions touch upon almost every aspect of the architectural domain. The functional aspects of a solution comprise what the system offers to the consumers as functionality to be accomplished. Non-functional aspects concern how the system can accomplish these functionalities, such as performance, availability, security, reliability, scalability, usability, and so on. IoT solution architects need to consider the scalability of devices, gateways, edge servers, cloud computing processes, storage capacity, the analytics process and applications. Interoperability means that heterogeneous devices and protocols need to be able to inter-work with each other. Connectivity is a fundamental requirement for IoT.

As IoT solution architects, we need to follow a solution method which can guide us on what steps to take, in what order to take them, and how to perform required tasks. Our chosen method can help us reach our destination most effectively.

Risks, issues, dependencies and assumptions need to be carefully analysed. Architectural trade-offs are required to be made for dealing with uncertainties. For IoT specifications, unreliable communication, slow speed and inaccurate decisions can lead to disastrous results.

IoT security covers both the macro and micro design phases for security. Security threats exist at all layers of IoT solutions. Therefore, IoT solution architects need to develop a comprehensive security document which covers the end-to-end security aspects of the overall solution at all layers and from all possible angles.

There are special considerations for IoT security and privacy. IoT privacy issues vary from country to country. The privacy issues are not always obvious.

An additional level of security to the application can be provided by using TLS or SSL as a transport layer protocol. We should never leave debugging access on a production device. One of the key authentication mechanisms of IoT is digital certificates. All communication between an IoT device and the Cloud needs to be encrypted.

We can introduce emerging and novel measures to IoT security solutions. Blockchain enables the smart IoT devices to control, monitor and automate with the secure and reliable approach. Blockchain is a distributed ledger that can record transactions amongst the parties involved in the process. Introducing Ethical Hacking to IoT solutions can be beneficial. Cognitive security is the application of artificial intelligence technologies that imitating human thought processes to detect threats and protect systems.

The security criteria can help us make a better assessment of the security risks. The assessment should also include consumers. IoT consumers also need to be aware of the security risks. The criteria should also include governance and compliance organisation. The OWASP Foundation provides useful security principles for IoT solutions. The IoTSF is the organisation responsible for the security and compliance framework.

Agile is an essential and collective approach to IoT solutions. Using Agile methods has become famous for IoT manufacturers, developers and service providers. Agile methods focus on incremental development and automating everything possible in the shortest possible time. Agile methods help the IoT solution architects to have a reasonably-manageable solution schedule. Agile methods embrace collaboration amongst multiple teams by breaking silos. The term Kaizen refers to continuous improvement.

A User Story is a simplified explanation of this requirement. An Epic can be defined as a group of work items that has a common objective. A Backlog is used to prioritise features and understand which features to implement in priority order. Sprint is a planned and time-boxed iteration of a continuous development cycle. Acceptance Criteria specifies the conditions that the solution must meet to satisfy the client. Daily Stand-up sessions are a brief status check session managed by the Scrum Master.

Performance can be defined as the amount of planned work accomplished by a solution in a defined timeframe. Availability can be defined as the probability of a solution functioning when required and under normal operating conditions. Performance and availability models can be visual, textual or combinations of both.

A top-down approach to IoT availability and performance is essential. However, an IoT solution also may require a bottom-up approach. Performance and availability go hand-in-hand when it comes to the quality of IoT solutions.

Constraints also need to be carefully considered for availability and performance. IoT devices require adequate hosting in well-managed and governed data centres. Monitoring, alerting, and event management solutions need to be part of the system and service management architecture. Since IoT protocols are evolving, their specifications may change frequently.

The amount of data produced by IoT devices requires careful performance, scalability and availability measures. We can simulate actual workload models based on the functional and non-functional requirements. IoT performance model mandates more data storage capacity, faster processes, more memory and faster network infrastructure. Not only is the amount of data produced, processed and accessed necessary, but also that it is shared frequently by multiple entities of the IoT ecosystem.

Every aspect of IoT solutions requires cost considerations. High-quality solution architectures can have a positive impact on cost. The cost can be reduced by making trade-offs with a methodical approach and collaborative input from business and technology departments using the Agile approach appropriately.

IoT performance problems can damage revenues. Service downtime costs can be very high and cause excessive penalties. Downtimes in services or defects in products can result in poor client satisfaction.

Some technological considerations can make IoT solutions more economical. For example, the Zigbee protocol delivers low-latency communication and is a low-cost and low-power wireless mesh network standard, while cellular IoT connectivity protocols are more comfortable to set up and they provide better reliability and cost-effectiveness.

Recommended Actions for IoT solution architects

As IoT Solution Architects we are action-oriented at all time. To this end, in this final section, I want to provide 50 useful action point that you can consider for creating highly available, well-performing, secure, agile and cost-effective IoT architectural solutions. The details related to these actions can be found in the previous chapters. This section serves an action-oriented revision of the critical points in the book. It can also be useful to create a checklist of these actions and review before starting a solution.

Action 1 Plan, plan and plan! We cannot overdo the planning phase, especially for IoT solutions. When emphasising the importance of planning, I refer to a smart, methodical and value-based plan. Not just random data crunching in project planning applications. In addition, ensure you have a single page business-oriented plan for your CTO or CIO who is responsible for the IoT ecosystem.

Action 2 Effective communication is critical. We cannot overcommunicate as solution architects. As far as communication is concerned, the IoT solution architects need to communicate at multiple levels with all key stakeholders. Communication can occur with the most profound level subject matter experts to the highest-level sales executives, and, of course, in between many other professionals. Both verbal and written communication is essential to produce successful IoT solution architectures.

Action 3 Create solid architectural models for Availability, Performance, Security and Cost. Ensure the models are approved by all stakeholders.

Action 4 Verify, validate and obtain approval for business, functional and other non-functional requirements.

Action 5 Be rigorous in tracing requirements to the IoT solution building blocks. While gathering requirements, embrace the Agile approach. Agile methods enable us to incrementally progress solutions.

Action 6 Make incremental progress for your solutions. IoT Solutions get more and more mature with incremental progress. When you complete the first Spring for a solution, move on to the next, and keep Sprinting!

Action 7 Be extra careful and consider all aspects when working on complex IoT solutions. Create a RACI (Roles, Accountability, Consulting and Information) matrix with the solution domains you identify.

Action 8 Deconstruct complex solutions to smaller chunks. Remember adding priority and category numbers to them.

Action 9 Prepare transparent and realistic cost cases by considering every aspect of our architecture and design activities.

Action 10 Create contingencies for unknown situations as there may be lots of unknown situations in creating IoT solutions.

Action 11 Be mindful of constraints and impediments. There may be additional costs associated with the resolutions of those concerns.

Action 12 Apply strategic thinking skills. Solution architects are strategic thinkers. This characteristic is essential for developing integrated and sustainable solutions. When developing well-performing, highly available, agile and economical architectural solutions, one must think strategically and be action-oriented, and hence act tactically.

Action 13 Add business value (such as contribute to preventing SLA breaches) by adding architectural rigour to your solutions. You can develop a dynamic governance model to this end.

Action 14 Approach the solution from multiple angles. For example, you can approach from top-down to bottom-up, from left to right, or right to left. Evaluate your view from each angle and obtain feedback on your evaluation.

Action 15 Pay attention to the usability aspects and make the IoT system layout as simple as possible. Make friends with the power users in the organisation.

Action 16 Consider useful technological contributors to make IoT solutions more economical. For example, the Zigbee protocol delivers low-latency communication and is a low-cost and low-power wireless mesh network standard.

Action 17 Deal with the complexity of IoT systems by deconstructing complex systems to smaller components, sub-components and elements, and then reconstruct them in your solution models.

Action 18 Consider the use of flexible IoT gateways to minimise the high volume of data generated by the sensors.

Action 19 Consider the use of Edge Devices for filtering and processing large volumes of data for efficiency so that the Cloud can work on the filtered data.

Action 20 Understand Fog Computing architecture for your IoT solutions.

Action 21 Consider the use of the IoT Cloud to facilitate data integration of the ecosystems to improve the security, availability and performance of the IoT systems.

Action 22 Use APIs to integrate devices, applications, data and the cloud systems quickly and effectively.

Action 23 Use the standards developed by various organisations, such as IEEE, IETF and ITU in your solutions.

Action 24 Use System Context as a communication tool for senior executives and business stakeholders so that they can see the big picture of the solution.

Action 25 Use reference architectures to create reliable solution templates and save time.

Action 26 Develop a comprehensive Component Model to explain the components and their relationships in a solution.

Action 27 Develop the Operational Model to illustrate how the solution can operate when it is deployed.

Action 28 Conduct a comprehensive Viability Assessment to include the critical architectural and technical issues, risks, dependencies and assumptions.

Action 29 Document Architectural decisions and obtain approval from a relevant governance body in the organisation.

Action 30 Validate Functional aspects of the IoT solution with relevant stakeholders, such as users of products or consumers of services by creating various personas.

Action 31 Validate Non-functional aspects, such as performance, availability, security, reliability, scalability, usability and so on, by considering how the system can accomplish functionalities.

Action 32 Create use cases with input from all stakeholders.

Action 34 Pay special attention to interoperability requirements in the IoT ecosystems, including heterogeneous devices and protocols to connect and inter-work with each other.

Action 35 Follow a solution method for guidance on what steps to take, in what order to take them and how to perform the required tasks.

Action 36 Speed up the delivery process

by customising it through the effective use of a solution method.

Action 37 Make architectural trade-offs for dealing with uncertainties.

Action 38 Factor in convoluted IoT specifications, unreliable communications, slow speed and inaccurate decisions in your solutions. These factors can lead to disastrous results.

Action 39 Analyse and validate security threats exist at all layers of IoT solutions.

Action 40 Consider IoT privacy issues based on countries as different nations may have different privacy requirements.

Action 41 Never leave unnecessary accounts open, such as any form of debugging access on production devices. Get them to check by a security specialist.

Action 42 Provide the most restrictive default security configurations on IoT product or services accounts.

Action 43 Use TLS or SSL transport layer protocols to strengthen application security.

Action 44 Consider the Blockchain distributed ledger that can record transactions amongst the parties involved in the process.

Action 45 Introduce Ethical Hacking to your IoT solutions to address difficult security situations.

Action 46 Consider cognitive security techniques to detect threats and protect complex systems.

Action 47 Create comprehensive security criteria based on the established principles from various foundations and organisations, such as IoTSF.

Action 48 Develop a comprehensive Service Management model for the IoT solutions targeting consumers for utility-based services.

Action 49 Validate Service Level Agreements in your solution and design availability, performance and security to comply with the SLAs.

Action 50 Reduce cost by making trade-offs through a methodical approach, collaborative input from business and technology departments and through diligent use of the Agile method.

Final Words

Concluding with these compelling actions, I appreciate your time and effort for finishing the book. Using these actions in your practice, especially before tackling a new IoT solution architecture engagement, can keep you alert for recognising risks, issues, and dependencies around your engagement. As a lead architect of the solution, practising these actions at work, you can set the scene, create the agenda, and lead your talented team with confidence.

I hope the guidance in this book can increase your confidence in undertaking complex IoT solution engagements. In addition to your architectural knowledge and rigour, with the business focus to reduce the cost of the solution, to improve the quality, and delivery focus with agility, you can be a role model IoT solution architect in your organisation. Wish you all the best and recommend you share this knowledge with your proteges who look up you as a role model architect.

Appendices

Appendix 1: Acronyms

AMQP The Advanced Message Queuing Protocol

BOM Bill of Materials CA   Collision Avoidance

CARPChannel-Aware Routing Protocol

CMDUs Control Message Data Units

CoAP Constrained Application Protocol

CORPL Cognitive RPL

CRC Cyclic redundancy check

CSMA   Carrier Sense Multiple Access

DAO Destination Advertisement Object

DDS Data Distribution Service

DIO   DODAG Information Object

DODAG Destination Oriented Directed Acyclic Graph

FDMA Frequency division multiple access

GHz Giga Hertz

IEEE Institution of Electrical and Electronics Engineers

IETF Internet Engineering Task Force

IoT   Internet of Things

IP   Internet Protocol

IPv6 Internet Protocol version
6 ITU International Telecommunications Union
L2CAP Logical Link Control and Adaptation
Protocol LoRaWAN   Long Range Wide Area
Network
LTE Long-Term Evolution
LTE-A   Long-Term Evolution Advanced
M2M Machine to Machine
MAC Media Access Control
MQTT   Message Queue Telemetry
Transport
NFC Near Field Communication
OFDM Orthogonal Frequency Division
Multiplexing
PA   Process Automation
RAN Radio Access Network
REST Representational State Transfer
RFID Radio-frequency identification
RPL Routing Protocol for Low-Power Networks
SDN Software Defined Networking
SIG   Special Interest Group
SMQTT Secure MQTT
SOA Services Oriented Architecture
SSL   Secure Socket Layer
TCP Transmission Control Protocol
TDMA Time Division Multiple Access
TEDS   Transducer Electronic Datasheets

TLS   Transport Level Security
TSCHTime-Slotted Channel Hopping
UDP User Datagram Protocol
ULE Ultra-Low Energy
WiFi Wireless Fidelity
WPAN Wireless Personal Area Network
XML Extensible Markup Language
XMPP   Extensible Messaging and Presence
Protocol

APPENDIX 2: USEFUL IOT LINKS

https://lora-alliance.org
https://www.thethingsnetwork.org
https://www.sigfox.com
https://www.iotone.com/usecases
https://www.iotone.com/iotone500

Other Books in This Series

Architecting Big Data Solutions
Integrated with IoT & Cloud:

Create strategic business insights with agility

IoT, Big Data, and Cloud Computing are

three distinct technology domains with overlapping use cases. Each technology has its own merits; however, the combination of three creates a synergy and the golden opportunity for businesses to reap the exponential benefits. This combination can create technological magic for innovation when adequately architected, designed, implemented, and operated.

Integrating Big Data with IoT and Cloud architectures provide substantial business benefits. It is like a perfect match. IoT collects real-time data. Big Data optimises data management solutions. Cloud collects, hosts, computes, stores, and disseminates data rapidly.

Based on these compelling business propositions, the primary purpose of this book is to provide practical guidance on creating Big Data solutions integrated with IoT and Cloud architectures. To this end, the book offers an architectural overview, solution practice, governance, and underlying technical approach for creating integrated Big Data, Cloud, and IoT solutions.

The book offers an introduction to solution architecture, three distinct chapters comprising Big Data, Cloud, and the IoT with the final chapter, including conclusive remarks to consider for Big Data solutions. These chapters include essential architectural points, solution practice, methodical rigour, techniques, technologies, and tools.

Creating Big Data solutions are complex and complicated from multiple angles. However, with the awareness and guidance provided in this book, the Big Data solutions architects can be empowered to provide useful and productive solutions with growing confidence.

Architecting Digital Transformation

12-step Architectural Leadership Method

Enterprises are facing enormous challenges to respond to the rapid changes and growing demands of digital consumers globally. There is constant search to find solutions to the growing problems. The most optimal solution to address this problem is to architect our enterprise digital transformation requirements aligning with digital trends and innovative frameworks as described in this book with an articulated 12-step method.

Architecting digital transformations address the root causes of fundamental issues that we experience in the digital world. The proliferation of digital media in the form of images, sound, and videos created a massive demand for our infrastructure to scale globally. Relentless sharing of these media types creates an unsustainable load over the networks, applications, and other expensive infrastructure components unless an effective capacity plan is in place.

Based on my architectural thought leadership on various enterprise architecture initiatives, digital transformation, and modernisation engagements, with my accumulated body of knowledge and skills from practical settings, I want to share these learnings in a concise book with a specific 12-step method hoping to add value by contributing to the broader digital community and the progressing digital transformation initiatives.

I made every effort to make this book concise, uncluttered, and easy-to-read by removing technical jargons to make it readable by a broader audience who want to architect their digital transformation programs to align with the growing demands of their digital consumers. In this book, I highlight the problems from an architectural point of view, following established and emerging methods, and recommend effective solutions to address them in a methodical way.

What distinguishes this book from other books on the market is that I provide a practical framework and a methodical approach to architect your organisation's digital infrastructure, applications, data, security, and other components based on experience, aiming not to sell or endorse any products or services to you.

A Technical Excellence Framework for Innovative Digital Transformation Leadership

Transform enterprise with technical excellence,
innovation, simplicity, agility, fusion, and collaboration

The primary purpose of this book is to provide valuable insights for digital transformational leadership empowered by technical excellence by using a pragmatic five-pillar framework. This empowering framework aims to help the reader understand the common characteristics of technical and technology leaders in a structured way.

Even though there are different types of leaders in broad-spectrum engaging in digital transformations, in this book, we only concentrate on excellent technical and technology leaders having digital transformation goals to deal with technological disruptions and robust capabilities to create new revenue streams. No matter whether these leaders may hold formal executive titles or just domain specialist titles, they demonstrate vital characteristics of excellent technical leadership capabilities enabling them to lead complex and complicated digital transformation initiatives.

The primary reason we need to understand technical excellence and required capabilities for digital transformational leadership in a structured context is to model their attributes and transfer the well-known characteristics to the aspiring leaders and the next generations. We can transfer our understanding of these capabilities at an individual level and apply them to our day to day activities. We can even turn them into useful habits to excel in our professional goals. Alternatively, we can pass this information to other people that we are responsible for, such as our teenagers aiming for digital leadership roles, tertiary students, mentees, and colleagues.

We attempt to define the roles of strategic technical and technology leaders using a specific framework, based on innovation, simplicity, agility, collaboration, fusion and technical excellence. This framework offers a common understanding of the critical factors of the leader. The structured analysis presented in this book can be valuable to understand the contribution of technical leaders clearly.

Admittedly, this book has a bias towards the positive attributes of excellent leaders on purpose. The compelling reason for this bias is to focus on the positive aspects and describe these attributes concisely in an adequate amount to grasp the topic so that these positive attributes can be reused and modelled by the aspiring leaders. As the other side of the coin is also essential for different insights, I plan to deal with the detrimental aspects of useless leaders in a separate book, perhaps under the lessons learned context considering different use cases for a different audience type. Consequently, I excluded the negative aspects of useless leaders in this book.

A Modern Enterprise Architecture Approach

Transform enterprise with pragmatic architecture using mobility, IoT, Big Data, Cloud (Revised Edition)

I authored this book to provide essential guidance, compelling ideas, and unique ways to Enterprise Architects so that they can successfully perform complex enterprise modernisation initiatives transforming from chaos to coherence. This is not an ordinary theory book describing Enterprise Architecture in detail. There are myriad of books on the market and in libraries discussing details of enterprise architecture.

As a practising Senior Enterprise Architect, myself, I read hundreds of those books and articles to learn different views. They have been valuable to me to establish my foundations in the earlier phase of my profession. However, what is missing now is a concise guidance book showing Enterprise Architects the novel approaches, insights from the real-life experience and experimentations, and pointing out the differentiating technologies for enterprise modernisation. If only there were such a guide when I started engaging in modernisation and transformation programs.

The biggest lesson learned is the business outcome of the enterprise modernisation. What genuinely matters for business is the return on investment of the enterprise architecture and its monetising capabilities. The rest is the theory because nowadays sponsoring executives, due to economic climate, have no interest, attention, or tolerance for non-profitable ventures. I am sorry for disappointing some idealistic Enterprise Architects, but with due respect, it is the reality, and we cannot change it. This book deals with reality rather than theoretical perfection. Anyone against this view on this climate must be coming from another planet.

In this concise, uncluttered and easy-to-read book, I attempt to show the significant pain points and valuable considerations for enterprise modernisation using a structured approach. The architectural rigour is still essential. We cannot compromise the rigour aiming to the quality of products and services as a target outcome. However, there must be a delicate balance among architectural rigour, business value, and speed to market. I applied this pragmatic approach to multiple substantial transformation initiatives and complex modernisations programs. The key point is using an incrementally progressing iterative approach to every aspect of modernisation initiatives, including people, processes, tools, and technologies as a whole.

Starting with a high-level view of enterprise architecture to set the context, I provided a dozen of distinct chapters to point out and elaborate on the factors which can make a real difference in dealing with complexity and producing excellent modernisation initiatives. As eminent leaders, Enterprise Architects are the critical talents who can undertake this massive mission using their people and technology skills, in addition to many critical attributes such as calm and composed approach. They are architects, not firefighters. I have full confidence that this book can provide valuable insights and aha moments for these talented architects to tackle this enormous mission turning chaos to coherence.

Digital Intelligence

I authored this book because dealing with

intelligence, and the digital world is a passion for me and wanted to share my passion with you. In this book, I aim to provide compelling ideas and unique ways to increase, enhance, and deepen your digital intelligence and awareness and apply them to your organisation's digital journey particularly for modernisation and transformation initiatives. I used the architectural thinking approach as the primary framework to convey my message.

Based on my architectural thought leadership on various digital transformation and modernisation engagements, with the accumulated wealth of knowledge and skills, I want to share these learnings in a concise book hoping to add value by contributing to the broader digital community and the progressing initiatives.

Rest assured, this is not a theory or an academic book. It is purely practical and based on lessons learned from real enterprise transformation and modernisation initiatives taken in large corporate environments.

I made every effort to make this book concise, uncluttered, and easy-to-read by removing technical jargons for a broader audience who want to enhance digital intelligence and awareness.

Upfront, this book is not about a tool, application, a single product, specific technology, or service, and certainly not to endorse any of these items. However, this book focuses on architectural thinking and methodical approach to improve digital intelligence and awareness. It is not like typical digital transformation books available on the market. In this book, I do not cover and repeat the same content of those books describing digital transformations.

My purpose is different. What distinguishes this book from other books is that I provide an innovative thinking framework and a methodical approach to increase your digital quotient based on experience, aiming not to sell or endorse any products or services even though I mention some prominent technologies which enable digital transformation, for your digital awareness, intelligence, and capabilities.

About the Author

Dr Mehmet Yildiz is a Distinguished Enterprise Architect L3 certified from the Open Group. Working in the IT industry over the last 35 years, he recently focuses on cutting edge technology solutions, such as IoT, Big Data Analytics, Blockchain, Cognitive, Cloud, Fog, and Edge Computing. He is a hands-on practitioner for solution architectures leading complex corporate projects and an Agile champion. As an innovation evangelist in all walks of life, he is also a recognised inventor.

Mehmet teaches the best architectural practices at work, mentors his colleagues, supervises doctoral students, and provides industry-level lectures to postgraduate students at several universities in Australia. You can contact the author from his author platform. https://digitalmehmet.com

9 781080 722969